A Bowyer Book

Published in the United Kii

by Bowyer Publishing in :

CW00346011

ISBN 978-1-9996273-0-0

Cover Image Extended Content License Agreement iStock – Getty Images

Credit Media Production

Grateful Acknowledgment to WikiMedia Commons for the use of Matrix on P.127

Author's Web Address: www.paquitalamacraft.com

Bowyer Publishing- A Division of Archer Business Group

PO Box 666, Eastleigh, Hampshire, England SO50 0PA

To Jeannett
from whom
I also learn!
with hugs
Paquita x

Foreword

You hold in your hand a book that will save you time, reduce your risks, and make you money. How can I make this claim? First, I've known Paquita for over twenty years, and I have been with her, as she shares her insights. They are valuable. They are inevitably practical, pithy and to the point. These pages are deeply grounded in her experience.

But there's something else. It does not come through in the pages as much as I would like, so I will tell you about it. Paquita has grit. Angela Duckworth, a MacArthur Fellow and professor of psychology at the University of Pennsylvania, introduced most of us to the concept of grit in her marvelous TED talk and book. Grit is the mixture of perseverance and passion. If you are building a company, your team will need lots of grit.

As a third point, Paquita's book captures the essence of our work at the Purdue Agile Strategy Lab. Gone are the days of pat formulas for building a company. There are no straight lines to success. Instead, you need to develop your own simple rules to guide your company. You need to find the simplicity on the other side of the complexity. This idea is not new. Kathleen Eisenhardt and Donald Sull introduced it to us in a wonderful 2001 Harvard Business Review article. But here's the tricky part: you need to develop these rules on your own. You need to design your own "bamboo scaffold", Paquita's wonderful metaphor for the task ahead. And this book gives you a really good start.

Finally, Paquita knows about turbulence. You will face it. And the only way to address the challenge is to move steadily through it. (This is where the grit comes in.)I teach this lesson to my students in agile strategy.

For years, I kayaked in the ocean off Maine. On some days, the sea was calm, the sky was blue, and the winds were gentle. But on other days, the sky would turn dark, the wind would pick up, and the swells threatened to overturn my kayak. The one lesson you learn with kayaking in a turbulent sea is simple: never stop paddling.

So it is with building a company. When you hit rough spot, reach for this book, generate some new ideas, and launch some new experiments to keep learning. This book will help you keep paddling.

Ed Morrison
Director, Purdue Agile Strategy Lab
School of Engineering Technology
Purdue University

Particular thanks

Shrapnel Free Explosive Growth emerged from many previous articles and short books written over a period of many years. In turn, these were formed from experiences in working with companies large and small to help them organise their growth. I am grateful to all those with whom I worked and from whom I learned so much.

This publication is the result of being able to take the time from busy consulting work at Archer Business Group - and I thank my colleagues for making this possible, especially John Ingham, with whom I work on many projects, and who was spending extra time on his book 'Spirit of 76: London Punk Eyewitness.'[1]

Thanks to my partner Mike who gave me tranquil space, tea, coffee and wine in appropriate order - and brought me flowers and chocolate biscuits to feed creativity.

My best friend, Balu the Chow Chow soothed me with snoring while I worked and walked me in fields nearby to clear my thinking.

Thanks to Nick Keith for his excellent and detailed proofreading and editorial suggestions. I always thought I had a good command of language but Nick's is the best! I also thank early contributions and editorial by Jonny Andrews.

For sustaining me through several years of turbulence that preceded the writing of this book I owe thanks to Charles Matthews, Jane and Greg Zeuschner, Marion and Paul Nash, Sharon Bristow, Robin Lamacraft and his family - and several other truly amazing friends who wish to remain nameless but whose support got me through devastating times.

My deepest thanks for ever more, to Charles Matthews and Caroline Baker to whom I owe my life when they got me to hospital in time in 2014 following an allergic reaction - and to Peter Woodward and Margaret McKenzie who had done the same in 2000.

---

[1] Later to transform his knowledge of the business of music into corporate roles focusing on content delivery technology, when punk rock first broke in the UK in 1976 John Ingham as a music journalist writing for Rolling Stone and other notable publications. He was on hand to document the very heart of the scene, famously conducting the first-ever interview with the Sex Pistols. He partied with the band and even bailed Sid Vicious out of jail. John witnessed all the first bands of the Punk era as they started, and with camera in hand documented the final months of '76 just before Punk exploded onto the world. His book puts this social phenomenon into the context of the era.

Margaret was Chairman of the Board to which I reported and once told me she made a long term investment in me. I trust she sees it as having been profitable for I will always be grateful for her faith in me and her encouragement as I scarcely held to life and in the hard following years.

Contents

Preface

When your very existence is threatened, you have to change.

This is one of the hardest lessons to learn in business,
because it's so counter-intuitive.

Plus... it's just plain hard to do.

Sir Richard Branson[2]

Too much reality

If you think growth is great, most companies can't cope with it. Here is a small vignette that describes the reason why.

You may not have seen this advertisement for an international delivery company. This is how it unfolds:

- A group of people watch excitedly as their online sales website is launched.
- The website visitor counter starts to register.
- From a modest start, the numbers increase.
- The counter climbs, steadily clicking over increasing numbers as new customers log onto the website and orders are placed.
- The team are ecstatic.
- Champagne corks pop. They toast their success, hugging each other in recognition of their achievement. The market loves them!
- The number grows, ticking over frantically.
- Glasses poised halfway to their lips, the group is suddenly quiet. Faces turned ashen.
- No one drinks. They stare in horror as it still climbs.
- Now already in the hundred thousands, the numbers fade into a blur: but relentlessly keep increasing.

---

[2] Sir Richard Branson grew his businesses organically from selling vinyl records to becoming a world renowned business icon with his Virgin Group controlling over 400 companies. Philanthropist, adventurer and supporter of entrepreneur growth, Richard Branson has retained an important aspect of character: authenticity.

- The sound of reality striking home hangs in the silence.

Without a word being spoken, this advertisement shows us some sense of what it will feel like to receive a constant feed of orders that swamps your capacity to fulfil them.

Success can be as much a problem as failure: a nicer problem in some ways, but no less - a problem.

This scenario reflects the biggest of all commercial start up fallacies – that explosive growth equals a guarantee of success.

The concept may be a winner.

The product may be a winner.

The timing may be spot on.

The market can embrace it hungrily.

But if you can't construct the sort of structure that will sustain all the ramifications of explosive growth, you have just had a preview of what the future may bring. It shouldn't happen to you. That is why you bought this book.

The reality remedy

Your company has grown fast. You hadn't really planned for this accelerated growth. Recently a few things not going the way they should suggests that you can't manage a company the size it is now the way you managed it when two or three of you made decisions as the need arose.

Or maybe you did know it would need some more structured organisation eventually - and didn't realise that eventuality would arrive before you expected it to.

But how do you organise something that has grown organically and has its own ways of getting things done - often varying depending upon who does it?

Or perhaps you are one of the few well organised people who do plan for accelerated growth before setting out on your entrepreneurial journey.

In any case, you realise that your fast growing company needs a different sort of organisation than the loose arrangements that work well at the outset.

What is needed in both cases is the ability to get enough organisation so that things don't unravel.

You need enough structure that people can get on with their jobs, knowing where the boundaries of their decision-making are - knowing what has to be done in a particular way, knowing why, and knowing how - or at least where to look for the details.

You want little enough structure to make sure the character of the company isn't stifled and that it can be adept enough to respond to the unexpected at every level of the organisation. We want to limit 'Systems' to the fewest possible

By having enough organisation to keep things tidy and smooth running, and little enough that it doesn't stop creativity and enthusiasm, you won't spend more time dodging the bullets of harassed customers and staff than doing the job you are there to do.

What we are seeking is to have a structure that suits your company. This won't be the same as a 'one-size-fits-all' standard organisational structure.

Your company isn't standard.
If it were, it wouldn't be growing at such a pace.

As John Gall memorably wrote in his perceptive and entertaining book 'SystemAntics'[3] first published in 1977 and still informing systems designers, researchers, scientists and others across many disciplines:

Systems get in the way.
Systems tend to oppose their own proper functions.

Gall goes on to demonstrate how a system starts serving its own life rather than address the purposes set out for it. We want as few systems as is possible.

You don't have the time to work it out in a complex way. You need simple - and you need to do it yourself with your team - because this is something that shouldn't be outsourced. It's too important. You might want someone to guide you through a process, but the work can only be done by the people who built the company to this stage.

There is only one reason your company is growing so fast. You are doing things right. Right for you may not be right for others but if it were not right for your company you wouldn't be growing and you wouldn't be reading this book.

You had a good idea. It's been well executed. You have the right people on board - but most of what makes it work is in your head. Use the winning combination that got you this far to build the organisation of the future.

In our workshops helping company leaders design and implement their own new organisational structures, we've been struck by the

---

[3] Systematics: How Systems Work and Especially How They Fail, John Gall. ISBN-13: 978-0006352556

richness of creativity that comes through from the teams these leaders have working with them. Your teams are probably no different.

You can read the content of this book and embark on this journey yourselves - or get help to do so.

Our company Archer Business Group has helped others reduce complexity as they grow - and in fact to find new areas of growth from what they already do, but so can many capable support companies and you may have a favourite. If the task looks too daunting get help - but you will have already framed your thinking from working through 'Shrapnel Free Explosive Growth'.

In senior roles with companies, and in directing growth agendas for cities and regions, I have been frequently surprised at how much time is wasted because of rework and 'work-arounds'. Although there were great Action Plans in place, there was no known system to make sure there were no overlaps, that everyone knew who was doing what by when, and why. Often the implications of non-compliance with limiting regulations or protocols were not factored into the plan - with predictable complexity of 'fixing on the run' as a result.

You note I said 'Known system.' Sometimes there is one, but it is a well-kept secret. Here is an example. I started out my management career in a Los Angeles office of a Silicon Valley start-up turned global company. My task was to reduce the almost 45% staff turnover and get both divisions to work comfortably with each other as parts of one whole and not two adversarial groups.

Now a well known name and a leader in its industry area, it was then growing fast in the technology boom of the early 80s. To help scale the company to multiple locations, someone (or probably many 'someones') had prepared a comprehensive series of operational instructions that covered all aspects of 'How To' for any office.

In recognition of the volume of comprehensive details within, a manager responsible for implementation of company operations was given six months after appointment to learn and understand the contents of this massive set of instructions. This book made War and Peace look like a short novel. When appointed to Field Sales Office Manager, I thought that if this was the baseline of operations I should know it on Day One. I did, and it proved vital that I had.

You don't need War and Peace. This book strives for something much simpler.

To have an adaptable but effective company as it grows, we want to allow a great deal of flexibility. We expect our team members to exercise judgement in responding to the unexpected so it's only fair that they know the boundaries beyond which they can't roam in decision-making. Sadly, many people wait until there are real problems before they force themselves - or are forced - to do some forward planning. Having bought this book, this is not you.

The examples in this book draw upon a wide range of experiences to guide you by using simple check lists. They are there to help organise your thinking. They may also spark your own creativity and that of your team. Accept such creative diversions. That is what will make your growth structure uniquely suitable for *your* company specifically.

As well as from examples gathered from reading widely across many disciplines, the case studies we use in the book come from a variety of individuals, attributed when used. Please send us yours. We'll attribute them too.

A bit of planning will give your teams the autonomy they need to free you to do the work that matters most to you - and to the company's success. It can't happen unless the bamboo scaffolding is properly designed and lashed appropriately to shield you from the shrapnel that winds of change can bring.

I wish you well on your fast travelling adventure.

Chaos is merely order waiting to be deciphered.

José Saramago[4] - The Double

---

[4] José de Sousa Saramago was a Portuguese novelist and social activist and winner of the 1998 Nobel Prize for Literature.

Chapter One

Bamboo Scaffolding:

Flexible structure and flexible staff

An architect's most useful tools are an eraser
at the drawing board and a wrecking bar at the site.

Frank Lloyd Wright[5]

You have created something that has a sound base. Even if it is still a dream structure in a venture about to set out on its course, the base concept and structure are sound. Now you need to scale small to bigger. It's not something we usually plan.

One day the many small things that have been going wrong, that used not to when the company was smaller, become a tide that is rising at a rate that could engulf the whole show. It becomes clear that the place needs a different organisational structure. It might even need to be broken into parts and each of these becomes a company of its own.

As you start to design the supporting structure for your own growing company let's offer an interesting way to do so.

Have you ever looked at the bamboo scaffolding used in south-east Asia and many Latin American countries when building massive skyscrapers and wondered: Why bamboo?

Bamboo, not steel, is a preference in areas of hurricane and earthquake tremors. It's not a cost issue. Bamboo flexes with the wind and the movement of the ground, making it best suited to survive the onslaughts of nature. It is also less dangerous a missile than a dislodged piece of steel.

This book will help you set in place the sort of bamboo scaffolding that suits your company. From its vantage point, you can adjust construction so your company grows in ways that withstand the hurricanes of change - the unforeseen battering created by the maelstrom of explosive growth.

You will be able to:

---

[5] Frank Lloyd Wright, architect, urban designer, interior designer, oriental art collector and dealer, writer and educator continues to influence architecture and urban planning long after his death in 1959.

- Design the sort of operating structure that can withstand unexpected change
- Hire people who will thrive in rapid growth and not be destroyed by it
- Inspire your management team to adjust management style and structure to keep pace with the needs of growth
- Deliberately educate your people to deal with change constructively
- Build and nurture your unique company ethos
- survive the extreme demands of keeping it all together while you work without enough resources
- Have a lot of fun
- Keep the team intact
- Make a name for yourself as a fair and preferred employer
- Create an indomitable market position

This book will expand your thinking. It is a guide. It's not an instruction book. Ultimately what you do with the information is up to you, but all these suggestions work: others have used them to their benefit.

Adapt, or adopt, or use the ideas as sparks that ignite better performance structures so your company can survive its growth curve of success.

There must be as many ways of doing things as there are people. Don't think this is the only way, or even the best.

Only you can create the best: because your design will reflect the company you are building.

As Salim Ismail points out in his book 'Exponential Organizations'[6], the more people and things you have to manage - the less flexible you can be.

Maintaining focus on the main thing is what you have to manage most. In deciding what IS the main thing, Ismail describes something not well known about 'Angry Birds'[7], the wildly successful game by Finnish company Rovio.

---

[6] Exponential Organizations: Why new organizations are better, faster, and cheaper than yours (and what to do about it) Salim Ismail, with Michael S. Malone and Yuri Van Geest ISBN 978-1-62681-423-3

[7] Angry Birds are multi-coloured birds trying to save their eggs from green-coloured pigs. The game is low cost and fun.

Angry Birds was Rovio's 53rd game. All their games were good but it took time to find the winning combination of design, end product, and ways of engaging with the user. This is not much different from designing a company.

*Early designs work but then you need to mature
into the optimal structure responsive to the times.*

Part of Rovio's growth curve was learning about investment and investors.

Early mobile phone industry structure required negotiation with 150 different mobile phone companies. As each company wanted 75% of revenue, more time was spent negotiating in this impossible 'Let's make a deal' environment than in the real business of games until Rovio made a deal with Apple and could get back to the main thing.

The Main Thing for Rovio was creating games. They were wise enough to recognise the distraction caused by interviewing partners for the Investment Dance and realising the Main Thing could lose out during the process.

It's useful to look at what other companies do when they grow. What works for them may not work for you, but there are always lessons to be learned - and it is always cheaper in every way to learn from other people's losses than your own.

Virgin's Richard Branson learned some vital things from his mentor Freddie Laker, who was generous with the lessons he learned expensively with the demise of his own airline. Branson offers these tips as you grow:

- Plan for the long term
- Stick to your founding principles
- Hire a great team, give them autonomy, and trust them with responsibility
- Get the right support

On that last point, as you grow you may want to list Virgin as a stopping off point in seeking support and investment for your own growth.

At the time of writing, if you are in the following groups, becoming a Virgin business might be a good option for you.

The link is in the footnotes[8]:

---

[8] https://www.virgin.com/become-a-virgin-business/step-1

- Travel & leisure
- Telecoms, media & technology
- Music & entertainment
- Financial services
- Health & wellness

Virgin is a collective of hybrid styles. Understanding the need to be adaptive and creative, and understanding how this is difficult in big companies, Branson's Virgin is a family of small companies - each autonomous - each successful at creatively manoeuvring through the challenges it faces as markets change - and each successful and profitable - or divested.

One of the keys of success is Branson's third point:

- Hire a great team.
- Give them autonomy.
- Trust them with responsibility.

If you do that and measure on results, not process, your people will take the creative solutions needed to survive and thrive. Don't let anyone convince you that a Strategic Plan for the next 3 - 5 years will do the same.

The holding company of Virgin Group has an adaptive structure under which these smaller companies operate.

It in some part resembles a classic conglomerate - a parent company with many subsidiaries.

With some of their companies Virgin resembles the Japanese 'Keiretsu' model common in Japanese manufacturing. According to Wikipedia, a Keiretsu is a series of interlocking but independent companies. There is a core bank and the member companies have small shareholdings in the other companies in the group. This gives some protection from stock market fluctuations and takeover approaches - in turn enabling more stability for long-term planning - something key for a company that has innovative projects.

With some of its companies Virgin just licenses its brand.

By contrast Hewlett Packard (HP) was often joked about by other inventive Silicon Valley companies of the 1980s as being the place to sell off the innovation you developed that didn't fit with your core business. The comment usually was "Sell it to HP and they'll set up a new division for it."

Too many divisions under a heavy hierarchical systems-based structure designed to cope with all those divisions - and departure from the early valuing of employees (The HP Way) for which the founders were well-known, plus widely publicised Board Room wrangles - have all contributed to HP's demise from a once top performing and highly respected company.

HP's best contrasting example to the Virgin model is that of the $14Million HP Support Centre in Medellin Columbia set up in 2012 - only to be abandoned three years later. Not having learned the benefits of small, agile, and autonomous, it would seem that HP is still operating an unwieldy and traditional hierarchy.

According to Near Shore America[9] , HP's published company statement on the Columbia closure read: 'These changes are part of a company-wide strategy to foster bigger teams with critical mass and concentrated resources across fewer locations. This strategy will leverage closer collaboration across the organization.'

Anyone familiar with the current HP Management structure will query the levels of collaboration that remains within HP.

I recollect their new leadership broadcasting internally that the goal was to beat IBM. Any company whose strategy is to try to catch up to another company has lost its way.

*Strategy is about developing and exploiting
a unique strength,
not about being a pale copycat of that of someone else.*

Lessons both positive and otherwise are always good to learn from the sidelines. Most of us learned as much by working in companies that were dysfunctional as from working in those that were models to emulate when starting our own.

In 'Exponential Organisations' Ismail gives us another great example, this time not from the English-speaking world:

Haier, the remarkable Chinese appliance manufacturer, has 80,000 employees and is enormously successful in revenue, profits and customer and staff loyalty.

Zhan Ruimin has been CEO since 1984. He broke the company into 2,000 independent, autonomous units (organisationally and financially) each paid on performance.

It's worthwhile to consider some of the structural characteristics of these units:

- Employees can switch between units
- Customer-facing employees have the ability to make decisions

---

[9] www.nearshoreamericas.com/hp-kills-medellin-global-services-center-blame

- Focus is to increase sales through improving customer demand
- Any team member can suggest a new product but the decision about proceeding is made by team members, customers and suppliers
- Like 3M, any successful product idea proposer heads the unit and can recruit staff from the rest of the organisation
- Any leader can be voted out at the quarterly review
- Suppliers, customers, and staff collectively search for new business opportunities using a common communication platform.

Having watched many great organisations and their success, I have learned a great deal. I also read a lot – predominantly non-fiction. This was helpful when, through Executive Search I was hired to put in place the organisational structure, processes and the right people for a 'fast growth' company. This was in the late 1980s. The financial markets were booming, as was inflation. Interest rates zoomed upwards. Financial Services Software was indeed a fast growth market.

I had no previous experience in Financial Services, but I did know the computer market, having worked for some excellent companies. I had also seen some abjectly woeful treatment of staff and their aspirations and the way their personal lives were considered irrelevant.

The MD told me he had read that companies change their whole structure, ethos, and needs according to their size. He believed 60 to be the maximum under which they could operate with their existing structure. They had 55 staff already.

Later study proves the truth of this. There are set numbers beyond which the structures of management need to change.

In the next two years, the company grew to employ 200 (another point at which studies show that there is a need to change the style of company operations) - and at the same time went from a no-profile company to one that led the market.

What a great opportunity: to set up a European Headquarters just the way you think it should be done.

Software companies, then, as now, were notorious for what is called 'Body Shopping'. Many couldn't care less about the personal situation of the person. They want a specific number of people in a specific location with specific skills, to do a specific task for a specific period, and they want them
there now.

There are realities that come with business delivery commitments that often have challenging deadlines that absolutely must be met. But there are also ways to achieve targets of time and profitability and still sustain the individuals who make up the company. This we tried to do.

At the time we are using as an illustration, it was very easy for permanent staff to vote with their feet and become contractors. Contracting pay rates were comparably sizeable to account for the loss of benefits and presumed security of a permanent job. For many talented individuals prepared to trust their own value in the market place, the fat rates of contract work well balanced the lack of preferential banking or mortgages some of the Financial Services companies offered to offset their lower wages.

As is usually the case, the people who became contractors were often the best at what they did and had the confidence to not seek long-term commitment. They knew they would remain marketable as long as their skills and reputation stayed at the forefront of fast developing technology.

The banks and assurance companies reminded them that as contractors they would have no benefits and the chance that they could be laid off tomorrow.

Of course this defied reality. In fact, many supposedly permanent people were laid off tomorrow.

But that is not my point, which is that you could lose your most qualified people very fast if they didn't feel valued.

Your own staff could also go to work for your clients. Of course there are such things as legal documents that are signed by both client and customer to preclude this, but in reality they are often scarcely worth the paper they are written on. When they are enacted by hefty legal cases they tie up useful time for key people who are drawn away from The First Thing (see later).

It happens: it happens a lot. You train them for the benefit of others. They take all their knowledge with them, including that about your company.

At the time this was an extra-ordinarily competitive market. There was not a huge skill base and everyone was competing for the same skills. In this context we created a company that truly could say: Shrapnel Free? No worries!

Our people could not be stolen away. They were fiercely loyal. They worked hard and played hard. They met deadlines - no matter what. They made constructive, carefully thought out suggestions about how to solve problems.

The harder things became and the more things went wrong, people got funnier as they reacted with humour rather than anger at the mounting disasters that often confronted us.

It was exciting, tiring, fun, extraordinarily frustrating, nerve-racking, and exhilarating - and a lot of hard work. The lessons I learned there are offered to you in this book. They are much cheaper second-hand. The point is – they all worked. But they all worked elsewhere - and that leads to an important note of caution.

If something worked elsewhere
– it worked in the context
where those solutions fit that company.

Do not underestimate the impact of context.

Shrapnel Free Explosive Growth is aimed at making sure that you tailor your solutions to your company.

Some of the examples in this book are drawn from that time. They are not the way to do it. They may inspire you to design the way to do it – for you and your growing company and its unique character.

In my working life I have worked with a wide range of companies, from small family businesses to privately held corporate giants - rural, urban and international companies - helping them position themselves with bamboo scaffolding.

It has been a delight to see the originality of design and the flexibility of the bamboo structures when built as 'one-offs' by people who had a passion for what they wanted to achieve.

So let's set the scene and help you select the right lengths and strengths of bamboo for your scaffolding.

Expect the best. Prepare for the worst.

Capitalize on what comes.

Zig Ziglar[10]

---

[10] Zig Ziglar came from a rural background, born into the era of the Great Depression. With his father dying of a stroke when he was six and his younger sister dying two days later, he was no stranger to adversity. Ziglar eventually became a successful salesman, trainer, company VP , author, and world renowned motivational speaker who lived his philosophy that you can't fully succeed unless you help others do the same.

Chapter Two

Charting a course: How to use this book

*If you cry 'forward', you must without fail
make plain in what direction to go*

Anton Chekhov[11]

Why did you buy this book? You certainly don't need any extra work. You are probably already scrambling to keep up. Time is something there is not enough of. If you are at the planning stages you are probably eager to get the whole thing off the ground. Time is of the essence.

Exactly. That's why you bought the book: to work out how to spend your precious time on the things that will be critical to your future and not be drawn into other distractions. You need to create flexible scaffolding within which your company can explode without taking out its supporting infrastructure with the shrapnel caused by lack of foresight.

The reality is that there is no Quick Fix. It will take some time. Not a lot, but enough for dedicated effort.

*The book can't do it for you.
You have to do it for you.*

Your company may be in the planning stages or it may have already started and be showing the signs of 'taking off'.

Either way, you have an instinct that you had better plan for the biggest success that even you can envisage.

In short, you don't want to be in the position of trying to juggle soot, just when the fire gets really stoked.

How do you start? Well, I am going to assume some of you already have started and you are like the people in the ad, but suffering not quite so much reality. You just have a sense that if you don't think it through you could have more reality than you can sustain.

Or perhaps you make a habit of planning for success and may just be searching for a quick and effective way to structure things under your own intuitive guidelines, instead of handing that responsibility to an external consultant or hiring someone just for that purpose.

---

[11] Anton Chekov was a prolific Russian writer exploring the vagaries of human nature, the significance of everyday events and how life teeters between comedy and tragedy.

You understand that people contracted to do this work are competent. They will institute systems that are sound and common practice.

But your company is not common. It's exploding in growth. That is most uncommon.

Consider that less than one quarter of new business starts are still in business after two years. Some may have been saved by bamboo scaffolding that enabled their management team and support staff to rapidly identify the problems and put a patch in place where needed.

But that's not us - not your company.

We'll institute the advice my Dad gave me about being successful in the business world:

Plan ahead, and carry your life-boat with you.

Your life boat is all the creativity and thoughtfulness you put into experiencing life. So let's start planning ahead.

Using this book
This book is designed to be used
- As a Planning Tool for yourself
- As a Planning Tool for the senior management or directors of the company

Some people do 1 and then 2.

Some prefer to gather the people who have helped the company get this far and set aside a day just to re-evaluate the current position and plan for some shrapnel reduction.

You probably already have bullet proof jackets on order if you have suffered the first stages of explosive growth. You can either wander around in tanks, or remove the reasons for shrapnel being fired in the first place. This guide will help you do the latter.

Whether a guide just for you, or together with your senior managers or directors, there are two dates you need to set aside right now.
- The day to go through the guide and work through the worksheets and templates, and
- The half-day to re-evaluate after a bit more reality has impacted your newly structured thinking about actually planning for success. We suggest that this should be six weeks away.

In the meantime, between these two dates, each person on the planning team can make a list of the things that need to be re-vamped, added to the priorities, or added to the whole growth equation.

You need to set in place a workable structure for successful operation of the company now there are more of you, and more orders to fill.

With your selected team members, get together to work directly from the templates. This will help you to construct your own creative bamboo scaffolding.

Let's set out our plan. What are we aiming to achieve?

The results we are aiming for:

We need to:

1. Describe the company look, feel, style, character, and ethos
2. List the jobs that you already have
3. Agree the jobs you need filling right now
4. Work out how staff will settle in quickly and become productive
5. Identify immediate needs to accomplish in the next three months
6. Note what needs to be accomplished in the next six months
7. Re-evaluate the mix
8. Draw the plan
9. Design the structure
10. Prepare the market
11. Hire the people
12. Introduce the newcomers
13. Sustain the staff as a whole
14. Have some fun
15. Direct the directors
16. Plan for how to handle things going wrong and how to evaluate and integrate a response to the unexpected
17. Create systems for awards and rewards
18. Share the wealth
19. Pass the baton

Strange isn't it? We think of hiring people as the first task. I've put it at number eleven on this list because I strongly believe that if you have the rest right, then describing the people you want is so much easier.

If you get the wrong people, you'll just be creating your own internal tornadoes.

Before we set out on a systematic design program that will leave you with your scaffolding surrounding a compact, well organised, flexibly designed company, let's quickly have a bit of background and context.

Companies that are about to, or have the risk of exploding in growth are responding to, or creating a market need. There are companies that do this solely in the domestic market and those with an export focus. Of those looking to export, some are what are called 'Born Global.' This means that their whole purpose from the outset is to serve international markets.

Some other companies grow from the local market outwards but have an export focus in their strategy.

If your company is Born Global then part of your growth strategy may be to look inward at the domestic market, using the credibility earned offshore to make market entry more rapid.

Either way, 'The Market' has defined your being.

It follows that taking your eye off the market could legitimately be seen as the first step towards a decline as exponentially rapid as was growth.

So, all the way through our design we're going to keep the market in our peripheral vision.

Research by the University of Queensland on founders of Born Global companies reveals that such companies have a learning culture from the start. Most are born from the adept transformation of new technologies and knowledge acquired in previous employment.

This sort of knowledge is constantly under construction. It integrates with other relevant partners
or products and is reconfigured as markets develop and types of need change.

It's useful to think about this as you develop the next stage of your growth – even if not Born Global.

We may not be able to control the market any more than we can control an inbound hurricane, but we certainly can lash our bamboo according to the direction and force of its impact. The whole construction is based on some primary principles.

You need enough organisation
so you don't have to think about
day-to-day operational details
when all your key staff are overtaxed
with the problems of fast growth.

You need so little organisation
that your people
can put their own stamp of individuality
onto the changes needed by rapid growth.

The rules need to be few and to allow for quick change and quick understanding of the change.

- You need people to settle in and become productive quickly.

- You need to record the conservation of every penny you can, so that when you arrive at that point when you are teetering on the edge of 'Go Ahead with Glory' or 'Bust in a Big Way' you can make a credible case for extra money.
  Those likely to part with your needed new funds will be more likely to do so if they see that finances and resources have been carefully used to address the real needs of a growing business, and nothing else.
  It's easier to do if you record it as you go rather than make an urgent backtrack over the paper trail at a time when you will have other things demanding your attention.
- You need what has been effectively called 'loose: tight' organisation.

We're going to focus on the essentials - the bare minimum of what will be the skeleton of your design.

There are some things we suggest you do not compromise on and some we suggest you do. But, ultimately, it's up to you. This is your company and your future.

We suggest you use a simple exercise book to do your planning. That way you can keep things together and not have to keep track of pieces of paper. It also helps you 'evolve' your thinking.

A book?

Yes. Not a computer screen of any variety: a book.

If you are doing this as a team - a book for every person please!

Write on the right hand page only as you go. This leaves the facing page for you to write comments on, add things, make notes later, and expand details. It also lets you work on the facing pages as you add things for your 6-week review session. So, with these things as the context, let's get started.

We cannot do everything at once,
but we can do something at once.

Calvin Coolidge[12]

---

[12] As Vice President of the United States, Calvin Coolidge became President with the unexpected death of President Warren Harding. He served one term and declined to run for a second. His policies have been viewed in extremes. Coolidge refused to appoint any member of the Klu Klux Klan to any senior appointment, appointed black officials, was an advocate of anti-lynching wars and granted full citizenship rights to Native Americans.

Chapter Three

Brand: How you stand out from the rest

*Your brand is what other people say about
you when you're not in the room.*

Jeff Bezos[13]

The company look, feel, style, character, and ethos

You may already have premises. You may be doing an Apple Computer style start-up from your garage, or be another Sir Richard Branson starting from a telephone booth.

You may be working in a loft, a basement, cheap office space in the wrong end of town, or smart suites in the best business location.

Even if your operation is a virtual one it still requires people to sit somewhere, interact with others, and even if virtual you need to have clear connections to your business fulfilment partners who may have to design, configure, package, ship etc.. Are they all to be virtual as well and only the core team is in one place – in separate places?

If the latter, how will the core team function?

How do you see the company two years from now?

Let's walk through that vision of your future company.

Remembering the need to keep the marketplace in our peripheral vision let's first describe the real essence of your explosive growth.

---

[13] Jeff Bezos, founder of Amazon and of the successful Space Exploration company Blue Origin is the wealthiest man in the world but states a quote on real values written by Ralph Waldo Emerson as his reality check and inspiration.

What market need does your company solve?

_____

_____

_____

_____

_____

_____

_____

_____

Why is your company so successful compared with others addressing that same problem?

_____

_____

_____

_____

_____

_____

_____

Circle the things that apply as you go through the following lists. Add others to headed lists in your planning book(s).

The face of the operation

Will your offices and operations have Physical Offices or be operated by remote workers in Virtual Offices?

Physical Offices

- Have a separate reception area that is wide and welcoming?
- Have a small reception area that is an efficient dispatcher of people and goods?
- Not have any reception area as such because most of the business is done elsewhere or online?
- Have a large sign?
- A small and discreet name-plate by the door?
- No sign. Like Skype when it started?
- Be painted hot pink, celery green...or in formal corporate livery?
- Security guards? Where, and with what mandate?
- Garden areas with barbecues and outdoor dining arrangements for corporate functions and for staff?
- Have an on-site company canteen, kitchen, chef, dining room?
- If so, how will it look?
- How will it be used to enhance your business?
- Subsidised canteen? How will that work?
- Sandwich van deliveries at regular times?
- Vending machine food?
- Cash or vend cards? (Where you have several machines that accept cash to be imprinted on an electronic card that is then used for all on-site purchases).
- Have refreshment rooms for staff with vending machines, fridges and microwaves?
- How will you stop it descending into an untidy mess?
- Have inside smoking areas? Outside smoking areas? Where?
- Good in all weather?
- No Smoking areas?
- No Smoking policy?
- Have open office areas?
- Have several small meeting rooms? Have full audio-visual facilities
- in the meeting rooms?
- No designated meeting rooms? How will you keep focus in meetings or deal with privacy or confidentiality issues then?
- Have plants? Your own, or plants-by-contract?
- Have pictures on the walls? What sort? Framed prints, original work from the local art college, posters - and if posters, what sort of posters?
- Who will choose them? If staff - any rules about content?
- Have cubicle areas for everyone? Open plan?

- Have private offices for executives?
- Have large, well appointed Board Room?
- Have feature presentation room that reflects the character of the company? How furnished?
- Technology?
- Will the place have a warehouse feel?
- Be busy, noisy, cluttered and fun?
- Be visually pleasing, showing good organisation, quiet but businesslike?
- Have music playing? Where? If so, who chooses? What volume? Background? Pops? Upbeat? Jazz? Middle of the Road? Vocal? Classics? Musak (heaven forbid)?
- Phones with unlimited dial out access? All or only some? If some, for what job levels will this apply?
- Internet access for all? Rules? Common sense monitored by...?
- WiFi everywhere for everyone? Are visitors included in the 'everyone'?
- How will they know the access code?
- Will your visitor access be within a firewalled area isolated from your company files?
- Will the team be able to connect any device from anywhere to your system? How will that work? You had better work this one out as it has become a norm.

Virtual Offices

- Where will the core team be located? Together? Own locations?
- If separate locations how will they link to keep effective operations?
- How will you link to your business partners?
- How will the website look and how will business partners use it?
- What is your payment system (e.g. PayPal or other)
- When someone is excited by the website and wants to buy, they want to buy now. This is the Web where instant results are expected. Can someone order immediately and get immediate delivery?
- What is 'immediate'?
- Will you have a back office for customer fulfilment and business operations? Where will it be located and what will it comprise?
- What about other aspects of your operations?
- How will you deal with each of these?
- Accessibility

- Have designated parking for all?
- Designated parking for some - and if so, for whom?
- Have a first-come-first-parked system?
- Have visitor parking? Disability parking is taken as a given - give it adequate space for a wheelchair user to manoeuvre.
- Have a few Staff 'Quick Park' bays for people who are just nipping in and out in 15/30 minutes or less? Will this be policed? How?
- Be close to public transportation?
- Be rural and require staff to have their own transport?
- Have a park 'n ride, a vanpool, a ride-share program?
- Be close to airports, major freight routes by rail or road? Ports?
- Work-at-home capability? Will it have Voice Over IP (VOIP) so that people working from home can answer the phone as if in the office, or some call-forwarding option?
- Will you expect your virtual team to use their own mobile phone? Yours?
- Is the reception of your service Provider good enough to accomplish that? Better check. They aren't going to use their personal phones and you want them to have some phone contact.
-

Production and Shipping areas and Operations area

Will they:

- Be contracted out to a service company?
- Be laid out by external professionals?
- Be designed by in-house staffs who know what is needed?
- A combination of both?
- Production fully computerised?
- Robotised?
- Will your warehousing be computerised with automated product pickers?
- If not, how will it operate?
- Reflect workflow sequencing to eliminate unnecessary bottlenecks?
- Operate in a Clean-Room environment?
- Be open for clients to see work in progress?
- Have plant tours?
- Be a tourist attraction in, and of themselves?
- Be used as a promotional tool (Like Rolls Royce or Ferrari where your individually-made vehicle can be inspected in the making).
- Have windows onto the rest of the offices?
- Be separate entirely?

- Have bays for more than one truck?
- If not how will you ship increased volumes as the company grows?
- What size vehicles?
- What turning circles will be needed?
- How will vehicle traffic connect with existing infrastructure?
- Operate 24/7? If not, when?
- Have staff access out-of-hours? On what basis?
- Need public access?
- Have an on-site seconds shop?
-

Products and/or services

Will they:

- Be online and link to non-virtual partners from whom you gain commission?
- Be wholesale only?
- OEM (Original Equipment Manufacturers) as components
- Will you have retail sales? Where and how?
    - On site?
    - Over the internet only?
    - Through telemarketing?
    - Through mail order catalogue?
    - Via distributors?
    - Through regional offices?
    - From your own stores
    - Will products be pre-packaged?
    - Be individually packed or be purchased as integral units?
    - Be able to be mixed and matched?
    - Need an on-site display?
    - Have distinct colour, shape, logo?
    - Be available in samples to tempt the buyer?
    - Have a refund policy?
    - Warranty? How will that work?
    - Have unique Point of Purchase presence?

Your crew

- What will the team comprise for the next 6, 12, 24, 36 months?

Virtual Operations

- If you have a virtual team, will you profile them on the website to give a 'face' to the company?

- If so, will you stick to formal presentation or light-hearted to reveal the personality of the individual through his/her interests and passions?
- When your Virtual Team members are required to make a business presentation how will they be expected to dress?

Non virtual

- Will they be casually dressed in whatever they like? Any limits?
- Wearing uniforms? Protective clothing? Food handling compliant gear? Specialist attire of any sort? Branded company issue clothing?
- Be expected to wear business attire? What IS Business Attire for your field of work?
- Are they friends outside work hours?
- Do they socialise together?
- Do they know each other's interests, families, pets?
- Do they tease each other?
- Are they diplomatic, harshly critical,
- Irreverent? Formal?
- Is there a 'look' you could describe about the way they dress?
- Does this image reflect what you want it to?
- Can Fido come to work too?

The reason for spending some time making the skeleton of the future jangle a bit less as it wanders through your present, is that in taking the few moments to think about how it will all look, you are making many assumptions that are automatic.

You are unconsciously designing a style, an ethos that will become the hallmark of your company. It may already have done so - with or without your notice. What it has evolved into may or may not be what you want. You may be describing what you want it to be, instead.

If you think that you are just another competitor in the market and it's not important to describe to yourself who you are, you may want to re-think the whole concept of explosive growth.

Who you are and how you act and look as a company can be a great accelerator to your growth.

In my sideline work as a copywriter I once went to a customer meeting with the team from the marketing company for whom I was working. I was drafting the New Employee Company Introduction and the Operations Manuals for a large global life assurance company.

The meeting proved to be one of the most surreal experiences of my professional life. I was the only woman in the room. This is not unusual for my work and has never before or since been an issue. Not in Abu Dhabi. Not in Qatar. Not anywhere.

On this occasion the company representative leading the workshop with his management team spoke only to the leader of our team. If I asked a question he answered directly to my colleague as if I was invisible.

The meeting was to use the collective knowledge of the various heads of Department to extract relevant details for both manuals. Eventually I asked about their point of market differentiation.

It was the only team I had ever worked with (in fact have ever worked with) who absolutely could not do so. After trying many angles of approach, in frustration I paused, took a deep breath and said very slowly. "Gentlemen if you can't tell me why to buy from you, then why don't I as a client buy from the Pru?" Finally I posed some suggestions and we extracted a USP that had some validity.

When I left the meeting my team were mortified and very apologetic for the behaviour I had experienced in the meeting. I was quite calm and actually thought it somewhat humourous.

My team leader said "Paquita he obviously has real trouble dealing with a woman in business".

My response was that this was not so. He *didn't* deal with women in business. I then went on to say with a satisfied smile that actually that really wasn't a problem as I had read that the company was in the process of a take-over/merger with Citibank. I pointed out that shortly his UK Director would be speaking with him and *she* would be asking him the same questions I did.

You should not only have market differentiation by being colourfully (even in conservative tones) unique. The way you behave must be consistent with the way you brand yourself. All these questions are helping you define what that is through the decisions you make on each of them.

We all love a story. The market loves to buy good products from companies that are distinctive.

Stand out.
Stand for something.

Or sit if you wish... but be different from the masses.

Image
What do your notes so far tell you?

- Are you the seat-of-the-pants high flyer with a casual, happily chaotic environment with only one focus: delivery of the best by the appointed hour?
- Are you a more formal structure in a more formal market place?
- Do you savour the noise and the interaction and feel that if that is lost some of the creativity that made the company what it is will go also?
- Do you recognise that there are times for the cluttered, overlapping workspace and times for a more open space, a more individual type of focus?
- Does the whole thing need to be carefully designed to comply with regulations?
- Will your staff be working on other people's sites and therefore have to reflect that company's expectations of dress and presentation?
- When your people arrive at another person's site do you want them to stand out as distinctively different?
    - More relaxed, casual, looking as if they enjoy their work?
    - Are there limits? T Shirts with rude slogans for example? Revealing dress more suitable to the cocktail lounge (unless it is a cocktail lounge!)

By now you will have a firmer idea of the look, focus and style of the future company.

How others do it
Southwest Airlines

Southwest Airlines[14] in the USA have a distinctive style. They were famous in the 1960s for their flight attendants wearing a uniform of hot pants and boots all the rage in the era. Now they foster a casual and relaxed style reflective of the individuality in their staff - people who they attract because they have personality and a sense of being able to add their own mark on the service offered.

Southwest reflects the same world their customers live in at any time: they *are* the era. They attract and keep people with outgoing personalities who enhance the outstanding record of company success.

---

[14] At the time of writing Ally Schmidt in Market Realist Apr. 28, 2017 reports that Southwest year on year growth is slightly down from 5.7% being just 4.1% in 2016. They have a current capacity growth target of 3.5%. Something works for Southwest, and sticking to their particular style of operation just might be what it is. www.marketrealist.com/2017/04/will-southwest-airlines-fly-more-passengers-in-2017

Fiscally secure by not over-extending their credit, Southwest has been able to be speedy and flexible in adaptation to vast changes in the domestic airline market. It is often used as the casebook for success in building a fast growth company that grew healthily - both fiscally and in terms of employee job satisfaction - and guess what? That has translated into brand loyalty and solid customer satisfaction.

Southwest has a distinct company ethos: so should your company.

Ready-Mix Concrete

When the cement industry was in a slump, Ready-Mix Concrete in Australia coined the term 'Think Pink'.

They painted all their concrete trucks Hot Pink in a country where being 'a bloke' was ingrained in the national character and before the time when the Gay Mardi Gras became a worldwide event.

Was it chance or creative thinking that saw a daily newspaper front page photo of one of the new pink trucks used by a staff member as a Wedding Going-Away Vehicle, the bride laughing on the footstep as her groom took the wheel?

Ready-Mix extended this creative thinking to understand the customer's viewpoint on concrete delivery. As the main market shrank, a new niche developed: smaller trucks for smaller jobs. Still Pink. Still distinctive: not just in colour but having the colour reflect the fact that they dared to step outside industry norms and the then accepted ways of responding to the market place.

Being close to their customers they identified an unmet need and snapped up and dominated the new growth market of Pink but Small.

The company has undergone many ownership changes since then and PINK has only been kept – or perhaps adopted by one company, Vic-Mix[15].

Based in the Australian state of Victoria, Vic-Mix are not only still pink –they have made the cement truck a member of their unpaid marketing team. Their website introduces you in a very captivating manner to their fleet of trucks: how they operate and – *what that means to you*, the potential client.

UPS

Brown! Who would think it could be a marketing coup? The dark chocolate brown, always clean and shiny UPS truck with its gold insignia entered an emerging market heavily dominated by FedEx with something that has always made me wonder. Was it an intentional hiring practice

---

[15] http://www.vicmix.com.au/Fleet.aspx

29

that the UPS men - for in early days mostly they were men, though there are now more women delivery drivers - were always equipped with a ready smile and a quick friendly word or two?

They were not devastatingly handsome (I guess some were) but what your mother would have called 'a nice style of fellow' with a pleasant personality, and great smile. Now that there are more women, the same may apply. Whatever the selection criteria I recall this as my first introduction to UPS.

In each of our offices the UPS delivery was eagerly awaited. I had to see for myself. In several US States the results were the same. It **was** worth keeping an eye out for the UPS delivery! Sexist? NO. People with the ability to be memorable because of an engaging personality of either sex are so hard enough to find that when you find a company who seems to hire for those qualities, you take note.

The UPS website[16] makes a point of explaining their business strategy. They have made a conscious decision that they will concentrate of the 'advantage' area of business. They have asked that difficult question of: Will we be cheaper or will we be the most reliable?

They aren't cheaper than FedEx or the US Postal Service, but UPS handle a larger volume of deliveries and like FedEx offer a money-back guarantee of satisfaction on US shipments. Note that both recognise what they can control and what they cannot: not a global guarantee – too many unknowns.

If you wonder about why colour matters in branding, on their website they actually say: Ask yourselves 'What can't brown do for you?'It's worth checking out the graphics associated with the UPS strategy explanation because they may have meaning for you in how you think about your future company.

FedEx

Mention the name and we can all see purple and orangey red. But do you know the history of this most recognisable brands – one that is often voted as in the top ranks of the most valuable world brands?

Originally the brand established in 1971 was slanted and in the same red and blue colours as the US Postal Service, with the words Federal Express written in full. The company was new. It needed to piggyback on well established credibility. The colours did that. The name 'Federal' also did that. It gave credibility by assumption of association and helped a small company grow fast by successfully securing government contracts. By 1994 the company was stable enough to withstand a brand

---

[16] www.upsteamtres.blogspot.com/p/introduction_9939.html

reimage and the current and enduring distinctive purple and orange logo was born.

Much has been written about the white arrow you can see by blurring your eyes a little as you look at the space at the end between the 'E' and the 'x'. This has given the FedEx brand a chance to lift itself beyond a brand to a brand with a talking point. Clever. The FedEx colours have also allowed brand sub-distinction by the fact that our familiar orange and purple actually stands for FedEx 'express' and with a red replacing the orange 'Ex' it represents FedEx 'freight'.

Coca Cola

In late 2016 in a list of the most valuable world brands, the list goes: Apple, Microsoft, Google, Coca-Cola, Facebook.

This reminds me of Sesame Street: which of these five things goes together? Unexpectedly, right up there with the tekkies, is a single non-high-tech company: Coca Cola. We can reasonably expect the most valued brands to be high tech companies- but not a beverage company. That familiar red and white label has existed since 1958 - and with white wave beneath it has held its own since 1969. The company ethos backs the solidity of the brand.

Coca Cola have long had a commitment to its local communities and to practical 'giving back.' Long-time supporters of the World Wildlife Fund, in each of their locations they support what matters in community building in that place. Despite this, in 2017 Coca Cola had slipped out of the top 10 to 13th place and in 2018 to 14th.

Brand value is not static.

3M is going in the upwards direction. In 2000 the 3M brand was 214 on the list of Best Global Brands. In 2015 they polished their brand to recognise their outstanding ability to invent. In 2014 more than 33% of their sales were due to products produced in the last five years. It is now '3M Science: Applied to Life'.[17]

Brand gives definition to whatever it is you do or sell:
use it carefully and wisely.
Brand recognition is one of the many tools
to 'Marketing without Advertising'.

---

[17] https://www.3m.com/3M/en_US/company-us/3m-science-applied-to-life/

Brand Protection

Companies spend a lot of money making sure that their brand is protected. For example I recall a big ad in a writers' magazine featuring a photo of a large piece of earth-moving equipment emblazoned with the Caterpillar logo. It read 'This is a Bulldozer, not a Caterpillar.' The ad would have been costly, but it was a regular. The reason for doing so is because if people start using the term 'Caterpillar' to describe a Bulldozer it is liable to appear in the dictionary as a noun. If it does, the copyright on the brand is lost, and so is all the brand equity.

'Brand Equity' is all the good work done to build a name for yourself as constantly providing good quality and being reliable, ethical, etc. Caterpillar offer a good example of brand protection at every level.

Maybe you see that company growth can come from linkages with companies who already have high levels of brand recognition, so your company gains increased credibility from the association. It's a good strategy - sometimes.

The approval process to associate your brand with a respected brand like Disney or Caterpillar is lengthy and extensive.

Big companies who have a respected brand don't want it tarnished by poorly judged brand association, so their process is very thorough before approving any such relationship. So should yours be when you get to that stage - but in case you want to link your brand with a globally recognised one, these are the sorts of questions you will have to respond to. They make a good blueprint for your company as it grows and when others want to associate their goods and services with yours:

- Is it consistent with our brand and our customer expectations of the brand?
- Is it safe and durable?
- Will it provide the same level of customer satisfaction as our goods /services?
- Is the company a leader in its field and one who has built its own brand well?
- Are the company and its distributors and partners financially sound and stable?
- Do they all have a reputation for standing by their commitments and being ethical in their dealings?
- Does the company and its supply chain have the capital and banking relationships to fund the rollout of the newly branded product / service?
- Is the company best in class for availability, delivery, and service?

Then, the actual product or service that is the result of the association should be sampled and tested rigorously before going live - which brings us to 'Fulfilment'.

'Fulfilment' is the term for the people who deliver your product. In doing so, they carry the reputation of your brand in their hands. They fail - it is not their company, but yours that is seen to have failed.

Not having a home-delivery distribution network themselves, a national UK department store with an excellent reputation for quality and customer service outsourced their deliveries to a national delivery company.

The delivery company obviously didn't share their client's careful staff selection process. The well-respected department store started handling an unusual amount of calls for goods that had never arrived. Not only did this mean replacement of the original delivery, it also damaged their name – especially when some of the replaced goods didn't arrive either.

Well, that is not entirely correct. According to later reports from recipients and their neighbours, goods did arrive: at neighbours, inside the chicken shed, or sometimes left on doorsteps to be adopted by passers-by at their whim. When goods went astray, it was the seller's reputation that suffered.

Are you designing or re-assessing the fulfilment aspect of your business now? UPS, FedEx and Royal Mail (UK) have good online resources for the small business owner. FedEx even has a free consultation option. Go to their website to check if it has relevance for you.

How your brand measures up to growth

Now you have a pretty fair description of what your company should look like in two years time. How does that image compare to how it looks now?

If you don't like what you see in the mirror when you are honest in describing your company as it operates today, don't look for another mirror. Fix the reflection.

Can you keep the uniqueness that has made it a great company at the size you describe? If you broke it into small units or even small companies serving the main one, would that work?

Jot down your thoughts as they occur on the facing blank page of the exercise book you started writing in.

They will be important to evaluate further as you gain more information about how to lash your bamboo scaffolding.

You built a brand.

It can spawn – or with some adjustment it can extend its current reach in clever ways.

Those choices are yours.

They will be made with or without your involvement, so best to be the Traffic Director rather than wake one day to a company you don't feel proud of because market influences decided its direction without your input.

Identities are the beginning of everything.
They are how something is recognized and understood.
What could be better than that?

Paula Scher[18]

---

[18] Paula Scher designed the brand identity for the Museum of Modern Art (MoMA) and has created logos for Microsoft and the New York City Ballet.

Chapter Four

T stands for Technology - not trauma!

*We are stuck with technology when what
we really want is just stuff that works.*

Douglas Adams[19]

If you are a fast growth company, you probably rely heavily on your IT systems. You may even have set them up yourself and that has been a key to your success. You may be the Whizz who designed a software solution which is responsible for that fast growth.

Forgive me for suggesting it, but you need an editor - or should that be auditor? I use editor because I am a writer, and although I am pretty good at it, I have always relied on a good editor to assess what has been written and make suggestions for improvement. You should too. In your case it may be more an auditor to assess the health and suitability of your current IT systems.

The more you think you don't need this, the more you probably do. I have spoken to many IT Support and Service Management professionals who can clearly describe the errors and omissions in the systems they support. Their astute recommendations are never heard. Management knows better - they think.

Remember the internationally broadcast indignity of England's Heathrow Terminal 5 opening in March 2008 when the baggage systems failed and over 40,000 pieces of luggage failed to travel with their owners - 23,205 pieces of luggage ended up having to be transported by road to be manually sorted and sent back again?

I do. I was there the next day – happily only with carry on bags on a business trip from Germany.

We met several Baggage Handlers: one was also a Black Cab driver; another was also a barman at the hotel where we stayed overnight. The story had its variations, but the picture that emerged was later confirmed by the Parliamentary Enquiry that followed this national disgrace.

---

[19] Douglas Adams was an author and script-writer with an acerbic turn of wit, who wrote 'The Hitchhiker's Guide to the Galaxy' originally as a BBC radio comedy, later published as a trilogy.

The failure at T5 was not of the physical baggage handling system itself. It was a classic failure of management, writ large. The Union is made up of experienced Baggage Handlers and their supervisors and they had tried to point out to BAA who operated Heathrow at that time, what aspects of the new system wouldn't work.

BAA were adamant that this was a sophisticated system and it would work. As my father would have said, a classic case of:

Don't confuse me with facts, my mind is made up.

Compounding that, there was slim planning on how to handle a situation gone wrong.

You'd think lessons would have been learned and many have. But when snow caused airport closure in December 2010, the same lack of planning showed.

Unlike Fraport that runs Frankfurt Airport and has efficient plans for extra food, entertainers, cot beds and all the small details to keep their stranded passengers in a state of as minimal distress as possible, this wasn't the case at Heathrow despite previous announcements that they were equipped to handle snow.

To be fair, unlike in Frankfurt, snow in England had been uncommon in recent years, and it was particularly heavy. However, as many airlines stated afterwards - they were not involved in the planning for Heathrow snow closures so BAA lost the benefit of their experience at other airports.

The length of closure was also widely criticised as being more a demonstration of inadequate planning than of safety concern - whether that later proved to be true or not. Perception being reality - it left the impression of poor planning.

Is there something about the way things operate within your company
that you keep hearing
and dismissing as incorrect or irrelevant?

Is it time to revisit that issue
with a willingness to consider the points being made?

The amount of rework and customer cringe that could be avoided by a regular health check and actually listening to the people who work for you is extensive. Find a way - and if you can't do so, bring in someone to take a helicopter view of your current methods and sit down with you and your teams to discuss improvements.

Now is the time to do this - not when you have created a crisis.

For many companies that grow beyond the point of management around one large desk, this becomes part of the organisational structure in the form of an Internal Auditor.

This person checks all the bitty details we've been listing and reports to management about fit-for-purpose status of your systems and methods - warning you of gaps or areas of concern internally, before you find out about them externally.

Failure of IT Projects

IT projects have an appalling rate of failure. According to research[20] on the period 1998-2005 within the European Union, one in four IT projects was abandoned because it didn't solve the business need.

Of those completed, one in three was delivered late and/or exceeded budget. The numbers in the US are similar and widely reported. This shouldn't happen to you.

Plan now so your IT projects do the job they are supposed to, at a cost that you can afford.

You note I didn't say 'within budget.' You do need a budget. But you also need some reality.

Budget will not account for the multifaceted nature of IT, its fast moving developments, and its interactions. In addition to the approved budget for a project, plan a management approved contingency that is not advertised and kept confidential.

This is the budget that allows for a cost over-run margin. Plan how this may be accessed and under what circumstances.

If you are paying due attention to progress reports and asking some hard questions en route, this may never be needed. If something happens that couldn't have been foreseen, you're not caught short.

Why IT Projects Fail

Apart from management being directly at fault through withdrawal of an agreed budget, changing the goal posts, obstructing or just not taking necessary decisions, or trying to control every activity within the project itself instead of letting the appointed people get on with the job, there are many common components to these failures.

However, the following things feature often enough to be evaluated in terms of your own business:

---

[20] A Study in Project Failure, Dr John McManus & Dr Trevor Wood-Harper: as quoted in 2016 by the British Computer Society Institute of Chartered IT.

The IT solution ill- matched to the business need

This comes from poor gathering of details of the business need driving the project and its relationship to other processes, company activities, and regulatory environment, and to other projects and activities underway within the company or externally but impacting the project.

Often business unit leaders are not consulted, or their input is not clearly restated to the technical teams and/or understood.

Inside management groups, even within a specific Business Unit, there is often a lack of detailed understanding of their user groups and their specific needs.

A large Nordic banking group were unaware that their Analysts had such extreme IT hardware needs. During analysis it proved that they needed to be considered at the same level as Developers.

Data Modelling takes serious crunch power and these analysts were making the day-to-day decisions on financial risk on which deals measured in their multimillions were being made, but their needs had never been properly noted.

Many projects don't make allowance for critical peak activity times when certain parts of the system are impacted - like assembling all the data required for the Annual Report.

Don't try and get sense from anyone about changing the system they rely upon for universally important activities at a time of their most intense reliance upon that system.

The implications of shift work not considered

In a major workplace transformation project within an energy company where there were teams in remote and sometimes hostile geographic locations, this wasn't understood - with predictable results.

On the same project, some teams were on three month rotation on site, then two months off.

This also had not been factored into the change so those not physically present hadn't been considered in the education about the changed system.

I have found that problems like this can be inherited by the Project Leader sent to rectify mystifying problems - but are thankfully relatively easy to set right before implementation.

Better to properly scope the project.

There was no Project Value Proposition

Each project should have one before being approved. What value will the investment of time, effort and cost bring in reward? Put more simply:

Why do something without a good business reason?

Lack of governance

Ineffective governance is not about one person having iron-fisted control. It is not about neat charts and reports. It is about clear definition of who can do what in what way and with whose involvement, and at what cost and in what timeframe over the duration of the project.

A RACI Chart is a good starting point. A RACI sets out for all relevant activities who is to be **R**esponsible, **A**ccountable, and needs to be **C**onsulted before decisions are made, or who just needs to be **I**nformed.

Like all planning tools, this is only effective if understood by all, used, and infringement is acted upon quickly and effectively.

The lines of 'who is responsible for what' need to be clear and inarguable so that in the event of a crisis you don't find all the fingers pointing at each other while Rome burns. It also makes clear who pays who what, why, and when. It means that meaningful performance indicators can be set and any disputes can be dealt with factually – and usually before they escalate to full legal intervention.

Poor Risk Management - or none at all

A large global company accepted a contract which had a package of client policies attached. The client was a global energy company and its internal policies were vital to its operation within tight regulatory environments in many regions and countries. The provider of outsourced services needed to ensure compliance with every one of these policies.

As these policies together with the requirement to comply were presented just before final contract agreement,. eager to close the largest order in the EU at the time, they were immediately agreed to - sight unseen.

There were supposedly 186 Policies - in 3 different languages. In fact this was incorrect. There were 222 Policies because there were Policies within Policies.

As was the case in this instance, six months into delivering an agreed plan whose design had not considered all of these requirements was not the best time to think about whether the polices had any risks involved when transforming the workplace IT systems.

There should be a Risk Matrix for any project involving organisational change (not just for IT). The Risk Matrix should identify all the What Ifs and show the agreed actions to avoid the risk, or in the event of the risk happening, show actions to be taken to deal with the situation.

Each risk should have someone responsible for it. The manager whose group will be impacted by a risk may not be the right person to be Manager of that Risk. Best it is the person who can engage the forces required to fix the problem.

There are all sorts of hidden risks in your operation. They evolve as you grow and reveal themselves when you find that your existing way of doing things doesn't have a method for dealing with them.

> *The best risk management is in empowering your team*
> *to respond to the unexpected and the totally unpredictable.*

Some risks are predictable. People are creative in their solutions and most of their solutions are very sound - but being individually created, often these solutions fall outside your control, placing operations at risk. The only way to discover these is to understand your IT User Groups and their unique needs.

Don't ask their managers. Ask the people doing the work. Their managers still think things are operating the way they were when the company was smaller.

Here is an example: Oil and gas pipelines need to be regularly inspected for safety. The process of sending probes along pipelines to inspect pipe condition and evaluate safety of operations results in massive graphic files. They need to be stored somewhere.

Engineers responsible for a major pipeline within a global energy company had no way to store this data within the existing system arrangements. Because this need wasn't understood, all this essential data was stored in ways that fell outside company jurisdiction.

There was no fail safe on this critical information. Stored on personal external devices, the data was frequently not backed up - and was accessible only to the owner of the device.

In another case, in the same company, the person who made all the recommendations for the product sales had designed his own software to interrogate the financial markets on the direction of futures as they related to the raw materials they sold. The results he generated were the basis on which all sales and investments of the global company were made. If something happened to him - poof would go the profits because no one understood the software - or had a copy of it, but him.

Risk Management is even more challenging when there are third parties involved.

*When there is a joint contractual obligation to deliver,
don't think you can't manage someone else's team
because no one in your company
has direct line management.*

*If their work impinges on your work,
you can, and you must.*

Every contract should have a clause stating that the contract team will abide by the agreements made in the Project Planning or Kickoff Meetings at the outset of the project.

This is when all team leaders assemble to contribute to, and understand the overall project plan.

This is where adjustments are made from input of those assembled who give a wider base of information from that from which the plan was first designed.

This is where the lines are clearly drawn about where each team's responsibilities for delivery and decision-making fit. There should be no overlap to these lines.

Planning should also include knowledge of any 'In Flight' projects (those already underway) that might impact the project at any point.

In your plan there needs to be an agreed process about how to deal with the totally unpredictable events that life has a habit of throwing at a well-organised plan.

Call it 'Resilience'.

*If not at a Project Kickoff meeting,
there needs to be some meeting
where all parties agree to the project plan,*

agree who is responsible for what, by when,

*where the lines of responsibility have been drawn
and how alterations to the plan need to be handled.*

All this is useless unless enforced.

Poor expectations management

Too often, from management to user there is a total disconnection of expectation about what the organisational or IT change will deliver.

This communication needs to be:

- realistic
- address the obvious concerns of each group
- show not just the benefits of the change - but how it will be implemented
- give expected timeframes
- start before the project itself starts.

The pathways from 'the way we did it before' to 'the way we do it now' need to be clear and have sufficient support available to ease the transition.

People find change difficult at any time, but especially so when faced with usual day-to-day operational deadlines and a whole new way of managing the information necessary to achieve them.

Project Creep

One reason your Project Manager needs laser-like focus is that project creep is notoriously insidious.

The problem is that projects are defined from the top and often the people at the work face 'just' want one more thing. The trouble with that is that this one more thing impacts several other 'one things' that in turn impact others. Before you know it, you have a project that is doing many things for many groups but in the process the original purpose has been reduced in quality.

Software people are notorious for 'improving' a perfectly workable component of the system that does what it needs to - nothing more.

Once 'improved' it is now out of the scope of the original project and therefore anything that it impacts will need to be supported - at the cost of the group for whom the person who 'improved it' works.

Your reporting structure should always be alert to things that indicate project creep so they can be stopped immediately, or as some would mutter, 'if not sooner.'

Database capacity

Need a database that won't fall over, crash, when your customers multiply like rabbits in an accelerated breeding program?

Check out uptimes of different operating systems. You will be surprised by the results. Perhaps piggybacking off someone else's system - like Amazon - may be a better option.

Maybe not. Now is the time to re-think your whole systems - not when the company is struggling to work so quickly and effectively.

Get some free consultation here too. Your computer system and how it works are worth your consideration. Do not pass this off solely to the 'computer people.' I can't stress enough the necessity for senior management becoming involved to manage capacity.

Look around at the big companies where reliability is everything. Why are many of them changing to different system platforms? Is their reason for doing so valid for yours?

If large and reliable databases are crucial to your success check out what Amazon, eBay, Ford Motor Company, Nissan, the big hardware or food chains you respect, have each done to ensure their own reliability. With your team discuss how that relates to your company.

What the IT people know

In making computer system decisions it's no longer valid for anyone to order from the most common name brands based on name recognition only. The term 'You'll never get fired for buying from Big Blue' comes from an era where management could defend a purchase from IBM simply because it was from IBM. That era has long passed. It is also not valid to go simply on what your technical people tell you.

Technical people know what they know.
They don't know what they don't know.

The computer industry is the fastest changing of all. The expertise of your own staff and their area of specialisation may not be still fit for building a system that copes with your success. Include them in the evaluation, but get involved yourself.

Be comfortable that the final decision has coped with all the scenarios you can conceive that could impact the company's ability to deliver at every level. It's your company and you know how things need to work.

Making sure your IT system is fit for purpose
is an operational problem not just a technical one.

The IT system is the tool to deliver
the result you and your team define.
It is not an end in itself.

No matter how fascinating new technology may be, the question is: will it deliver with fast growth?

Get genuine inquisitiveness by assuring your own people that they will be trained on anything new that is selected - and at your cost.

"Good grief," you say. "Our cost?"

If not, why would your own team recommend something that may put them out of a job: even if it is the best solution to your growth problems? Also, be honest. Perhaps it was your own company that systematically de-skilled them. Seems only fair to redress that.

If your computer network or database is crucial to your continued effective growth, then you may have to make this investment.

The alternative is to do the evaluation alone. It's your choice. It's your company and your budget. But someone has to run the thing, and if the people you have are the right people with the wrong skills, you have a choice.

Possible solutions

- You could team them with someone who has the skills who is hired specially for this purpose. That way you don't lose the company knowledge so essential to tailoring effective integration of any new system.
- You can train them. You can show them that you are prepared to add a whole new skill set to their resume at your cost, and get them excited.
- You can move them to other roles.

There are lots of options. Ask questions. Project the biggest numbers you can think of, and then triple them.

Ask what response times should be expected, and expect to be given real examples. When you are satisfied with this answer, triple the numbers again and ask the same question.

Ask how transactions are processed and get a roadmap drawn - a storyboard of how your IT systems respond to the current business being done.

Then ask how these systems could be adapted to new business. If no one has thought about that, they should - and you should be involved in the final answer - or at least in the scoping of what is needed.

The business need was misunderstood

Taking the time to really scope the problems that are to be solved and inter-relating them across your whole system is the job of your Systems Architect - but as a reference point get her to explain how that all works.

If you as the business leader can see that not all contingencies have been addressed, talk it through. You don't need to understand the thing in detail but you should be able to look at the roadmap and recognise that necessary interactions are in place.

Keep your controlling thoughts at bay. This is her job, not yours. All you need to know is that things aren't working in isolation. Find reports that give you key data in a way you understand, but I reiterate: don't try to paddle.

You are there to steer.

Take the paddle away from the team leader and you'll all go over the rapids.

Depending on the IT Expert

Your daughter is a computer whizz.
She grew up with computers.
She is a Digital Native.
She is an expert.

Whether it is your daughter, son, Aunty Harriet's best friend or neighbour - don't believe that just because they are so-called Digital Natives and grew up with an iPad or iPhone this means that they understand computers.

They usually don't. Neither do the people you employ of the same generation - unless they have undergone some specific training.

It's worth remembering that earlier computer users needed to know the difference between storage and memory.

They came to understand the hierarchical method of file storage on the hard drive, and that memory has its limitations.

Not understanding these basics creates a 'cause and effect disconnect' that can leave your company data at risk.

In a terrific article by Mike Elgan in Forbes Magazine[21] he points out that as using a computer becomes easier and easier, there is no cause for curiosity about why things work.

Users of applications just look for another app rather than using logic to work through the solution to the need.

Without specific training most Digital Natives are used to using something but not in building something, so thinking through the

---

[21] Forbes Magazine Nov 14,2013 (and the situation hasn't improved by 2017)
www.forbes.com/sites/netapp/2013/11/14/kids-cant-compute-problem/#4f7748c131d1

relationship between a business need and a way to represent that effectively in design of a solution is alien.

In short, Digital Natives
who are not trained to do otherwise,
fit the task to the tool.

You need to have people fit the right tool to the task.

Consultants might well be like your daughter the IT wizard! Check their previous success.

Hiring competent and suitable people

How do you hire people for IT? If this process doesn't include some testing you're putting yourself at risk of hiring someone without the skills – or aptitude - to do the job.

Testing might mean hiring someone you believe fits and letting them demonstrate their skills over their probationary period.

Applicants should be tested to see if their answers display an understanding of the thinking required to achieve the task, even if they are unfamiliar with the precise language or environment.

A recent straw poll of IT professionals done by us in one of our assignments asked the value of testing in employment interviews. The results were unanimous and can best be summarised like this: Testing is only useful when you find ways to see if someone can actually *DO* what needs to be done.

They all said that they often were self taught and might not know the 'proper' name for something they used daily. Also, they knew *HOW* to do something within a specialty but might not have the exact routine of where to start precise...but they knew where to look.

One person explained a series of test that were of the sort where you had to work out which number came next given a group of seemingly random numbers.

The next test was on shapes and what was the next logical shape that would follow the last of a similarly seemingly random test.

I said that this should have suited his mathematical mind and systems architect thinking. He didn't think so. He found the tests very difficult. I asked what he did about that. The answer?

"I figured that they were testing my ability to think reasonably given what information I had. If I am in front of a client as the technical person I can't dither – so I made a decision". He got the job. The hiring company actually paid him considerably more than his current salary and said they knew they were, but "This is what you are worth to us". That is a company who knows who will fit.

*Hire for the ability to think things through
in an intelligent fashion.*

IT Cost

Is the most commonly used and most expensive the best?
Remember that it doesn't have to be fancy, it doesn't have to be the latest,
but it does need to be demonstrably reliable and to work for the things
that your company needs.

In times of explosive growth every penny needs to be carefully
invested. That doesn't say buy cheap. It says buy tailored to need and for
value of result.

In that fast growth Silicon Valley company whose Los Angeles
sales office I managed in the 1980s, did I mention Edwards Air Force
Base? This was the era of the Apple IIe and the very first IBM PC.

The software was designed in our office in that era is responsible
for some of the most amazing star shot images only now reaching us from
the satellites sent up then.

*It doesn't have to be the latest or the fanciest.
It just has to do the job it is meant to do.*

In that fast growth Financial Services Software company I
mentioned before, we operated all Human Resources functions on a
simple software program that sold in the US for less than $100 and less
than £90 in the UK.

Before making that decision, I evaluated a magnificent, integrated,
modular personnel management and payroll system. It did everything. It
was wonderful. The only problem with it was that it was designed for
companies the size of Marks and Spencer and British Telecom. In
metaphorical terms, their size dictated that they needed the equivalent of
a whole room. We just needed the equivalent of the light switch! But just
like them we would have to buy the modules one by one to a total cost
equivalent to over £250,000.

My proposal following this evaluation was accepted.
I made the case that the records of up to 200 staff could fairly easily be
migrated to a new system when we had the need and the financial
resources to do so. In the meantime, I proposed that this Mom and Pop
Shop software would do the job. It did!

Perhaps for you too there are not so shiny and new but perfectly
functional solutions to your growing business needs.

Actually, there was one rather major glitch with the Mom and Pop
Shop software but it was, like many problems with computers - a user
problem, not a software problem, although I suppose it may have been

impossible for this to happen with the £250,000 version. However, I am sure you will recognise the type of scenario I am about to describe:

I had expressly stated that the new boy-wonder in-house computer support chaps were not to touch any of the computers in my group without my involvement. This was because I had watched them work elsewhere.

Remember the Digital Natives caution? This predates it but has similar elements. My reason for the ban was that in my presence in another department the technician had started 'repairing' the system.

For those of us who are computer dinosaurs or those well trained since then, it is considered standard to always have a copy from which you can reinstall the original 'just in case'.

The new chaps were eager and 'knew things'. They didn't use this simple standard and I saw this when they didn't note down their procedures with an old-fashioned pen and paper as they navigated uncharted territory so they could follow the crumbs back to Hansel and Gretel's safe house if they got lost in the woods.

One day a tiny and very charmingly chic French secretary appeared in my doorway with a very tentative manner to announce that the new chaps had overwritten the holiday database. I raised an eyebrow and said calmly that this should be no problem as they could just reinstall the backup copy.

I knew that she wouldn't be standing there looking crestfallen if they had done so - but the error did require a bit of suitably felt concern about consequences by those who had allowed two of the very few 'thou shalt nots' of our team to be ignored:

Thou shalt not fail to back up – and thou shalt not allow enthusiastic technical support people to operate unsupervised on critical data before their training overcame this fault in their procedures.

When advised that indeed there was no backup, I paused and looked out at the canal boats chugging slowly past my window. It was just a small pause but I am sure an uncomfortable one. Looking back at the crestfallen person, I replied: 'It's just as well that I have one then, isn't it'?

I always follow the 'Trust your mother but cut the cards' rule. This means having faith in the system but making precautions that cover the remote chance of its failure.

Learn from rock climbers:
If something is critical, employ three points of contact.

In this case my three points of contact were: It's critical – so therefore you have a copy, the system has a copy - and I have a copy 'just in case.

During the Blitz in London in World War II, Phyllis, the secretary-cum bookkeeper for Jack Cohen used this rule as well. It may have changed the course of UK supermarket history, and I tell it to you as Phyllis told it to me.

Jack sold surplus groceries from a stall in the East End of London and then they started a small office.

The books recording all his transactions were all kept in the office overnight but when the War turned to British shores Phyllis decided at the start of the Blitz of London in World War II that they were too valuable to be lost. These held all Jack Cohen's vital contacts and accounts: years of carefully kept records. Therefore, without telling anyone, Phyllis always took a copy with her to her own home which was marginally away from the site of the main bombing raids.

One night in the firebombing of the East End, the office was razed to the ground. In the morning a distraught Jack stood outside when she arrived, shaking his head. Phyllis took the books from her carryall - she had saved all his records.

Who was Jack Cohen?

Founder of an empire. In 1924 after buying a shipment of tea from a gentleman called T.E.Stockwell, Mr. Cohen had sent Phyllis to register a company name that combined the letters of Stockwell's name to be TESCO, the now giant supermarket chain.

Make sure there are copies
and a way to revert to a former version of your system.

...and check your automated backup. If files are stored in the places the backup system doesn't know about – they're on their own and a presumed back-up may in fact not be taking place at all.

Outsourcing

Is there a better Return on Investment by outsourcing your IT? If you think so, get some opinions on both side of the case - then make your own decision.

IT Changes

A cautionary note: A loyalty card offered by a large supermarket chain initially only for fuel purchases above a small amount only drew a small number of subscribers.

To build uptake, management decided to expand loyalty points to every purchase in every department of the store, not just for fuel.

The result was great: Huge uptake. Very quickly the exponential take up of the loyalty offer had unexpected consequences. With this sudden and large expansion of users on a system that had been growing incrementally at a respectable pace, IT systems crashed.

Databases already at capacity were suddenly no longer fit for-purpose. No one had bothered to mention the change in marketing to the IT team who could have suggested that a bit of prior planning would save embarrassment.

Without effective capacity management, it didn't!

There should be a way that changes are passed through a check system before going live... and 'Check System' doesn't mean as it does in a company with rather more than its share of complications caused by 'mates' deals within the company and with the external supply chain.

These arrangements mean that there is no internal discipline for poor performance because there is no discipline allowed to be enacted when cause and effect results in really damaging results.

This company is a regional UK Plumbers Merchant. The head of IT makes changes over the weekend (actually – he takes the changes made by others and 'improves them') and puts them live to the system on Monday.

In this case, there is no independent review of changes and their potential impact on other dependencies. No one has the opportunity to review and add a cautionary note about possible impacts.

Memorably, using this process of godlike omnipotence, this chap overwrote the whole live system. It meant a day of no access at any till in their chain until they restored a previous copy (which should have been able to be done immediately, but wasn't, because those breadcrumbs along the pathway had all been erased in the course of the changes made – and there was no baseline to which one could safely return). The manual entries of the day's transactions had to be then entered (also manually) over the following days.

To prevent this sort of damage, most companies have a 'sand box' which emulates the live system and where changes are tested. The reasons for isolating the test system from the one the company is using to get the day's job done needs no further explanation.

Licensing

If you don't have someone in charge of licensing, you should. This doesn't just mean making sure licenses are renewed on their required dates, or that they are upgraded when they exceed agreed terms of use such as number of users.

Licenses for software applications often have cautionary clauses that say the license is only good if their application runs on the hardware, operating system or platform as listed in the License Agreement.

Half way into an IT transformation or upgrade of hardware is not the time to discover that suddenly your key applications don't work - or are working illegally.

Hardware Refresh

Do you have a refresh cycle for your equipment?
What should be the duration of the hardware refresh? There is no correct single answer. Too soon, and you spend money before you have to. Too late, and you risk the whole operation coming to a sudden and embarrassing halt.

It depends on the needs of the business -and the generally accepted 'between 2-5 years' might not even be right for your company.

Systems Audit

When did you last have an IT computer system audit?

It should have listed the processor power, I/O (Input/ Output) and bus speeds and memory of the servers. This will help you work out your storage capacity and give some indication of a fit-for-purpose cycle to ensure new services are able to be supported.

These are what should periodically be assessed to ensure harmony with business need and expectation and capacity to deliver, but don't leave out the one thing that may be the most telling: User Satisfaction.

Several years ago I was witness to a major not-for-profit organisation's User Satisfaction Survey. They had a 4% user satisfaction. The four did not represent any missing zeros. Not 40% but 4%.

The reward for this level of total misunderstanding of the needs of their users was such that when the organisation split into two autonomous units guess who was put in charge of designing the new system to support each group. It defied belief. But that is what happens when things get too big to manage elegantly.

Elegant means shedding everything superfluous
and ending up with streamlined and functional.

Elegant should prove pleasing to those who encounter it
in whatever capacity they do.

The real culprit for this sort of damage is usually a rewards system based on process and not result.

Remember Gall's comments mentioned earlier? The system starts to serve itself, not its actual purpose.

Don't fall into the trap of not checking how your IT system is serving the changed business needs of today – and the expected changes of the foreseeable future. Your own staff are best judges of this but best evaluate it systematically.

This what an IT systems audit should encompass:

- A high-level systems architecture review – this is your map of your core system and its main components and interfaces.
- Business process mapping – does it deliver what users need to do their jobs? Needs change. What was fit for purpose before may not be now.
- User identity management – making sure the right people have the right access to get the right access at the times when it might be needed (according to their definition – not yours)
- Operating systems settings – this is what becomes immediately available to a group of users that sit under a specific umbrella so they are instantly operationally enabled. There should be fewer of these than more – and if these standard settings per group are constantly tinkered with – you really have shrapnel shedding throughout your workplace because that means your groups are not all working to a common standard and their output cannot be equally measured nor can they respond to your clients in the way you expect. *For example the teams in France might have 'just' made changes that the team in Germany hasn't. Communications effectiveness across offices then becomes something rather greater than being a problem of cultural and language differences.*
- Security controls for applications
- Database access controls (e.g. database configuration, account access, roles defined in the database)
- Anti-virus/Anti-malware controls
- Network controls how ell your configurations on switches and routers, use of Access control lists, and firewall rules all measure up to *current business needs*
- Logging and auditing systems and processes
- IT privileged access control (e.g. System Administrator or root access)
- IT processes in support of the system (e.g. user account reviews, change management)
- Backup/Restore procedures
- Disaster Recovery procedures

How cost effective is 'Cost Effective'?

Consider the Total Cost of Ownership
and not just the price per unit.

This will include the cost:benefit ratio of smaller vs. larger physical footprint, energy usage, cooling requirements, etc. Perhaps Virtual Machines should feature in your inventory.

Does a major shift in technology really have impact on you or not?

Many people in management fall to the ruse of 'Thou shalt' that masquerades as a need to respond to major shifts in technology.

It's like delegating. You delegate when something is going to happen a lot and it is taking up too much of your time— or when it becomes out of your field of expertise, so it is worth investing time to hand over the reins effectively.

You don't delegate when the thing you are delegating is of a nature that it happens so rarely that it will take more time to set up a properly skilled delegate than to do it yourself.

It's not a bad measure for whether new technology is really going to deliver what those enamoured of it say it will and why they feel your company is compelled to respond with positive uptake.

They may be right. It might also be a case of your company needing the light switch and a corporate needing the whole room.

Make the case for your business, not on what the analysts or consultants tell you to be the norm 'for business these days' - or heaven forbid 'Best Practice.'

Best Practice is history - you are the future.

Best Practice was best practice
where it suited the context of where it proved best.

Your company is not that place.

Cloud partners are not always angels

Consider accessing new leaner technology through a cloud partner. This is their primary business and keeping their servers up to date and operational becomes their problem, not yours.

Be cautious about outsourcing apply here as well.

You manage any such partner, not they you.

Disruptive Change caused by new technologies

If you are in manufacturing, or manufacturing affects your market sector, have you considered the impact of:

- 3D manufacture and laser metal sintering
- Industry 4.0
- The interconnectedness of the Internet of Things?
- Bitcoin
- Blockchain

These will impact the way your future IT must be structured, whether you believe that today, or not.

Do some research.

Regulatory Compliance and IT

The quagmire of compliance was always a sticky one. Its stickiness has got worse and continues to do so.

Whatever your sector or industry sector of the clients you serve, the need for Regulatory Compliance is almost outstripping the capability to meet it.If you haven't recently checked the regulatory environment that affects your business you should. According to findings of the 2016 Thomson Reuters[22] 'Cost of Compliance Report,' the big three that impact business the most are: Compliance Monitoring, Regulatory Reporting, and Capturing Regulatory Change.

Perhaps this falls to an Internal Audit - that group you don't have now but may want to consider having, depending upon the complexity and risks associated with your business and the market it serves.

If you outsource this to professionals whose living depends upon being absolutely up to date, make sure you are indemnified so if things go wrong due to whatever advice they gave and upon which you acted, the penalties lie at their door and not yours.

In some regulatory environments that isn't possible: the responsibility lies directly with management.

Before you can even know that risk, someone in your organisation should understand the current regulatory compliance requirements that impose on your business.

---

[22] Thomas Reuters 'FinTech, RegTech and the role of compliance' published on 5 Dec 2016 by Susannah Hammond www.blogs.thomsonreuters.com/answerson/fintech-regtech-compliance

If you think you are still small and compliance is something that your IT system doesn't need to handle, consider a UK Compliance issue that now applies to all small businesses - even the window cleaner who has his brother working with him.

Although a British example, this is indicative of the sorts of changes to regulations that are appearing regularly on the small business horizon in many countries. Our example case is the need to manage the update to the Automatic Enrolment applied to the 2008 Workplace Pensions Act.

Enrolment of employees needed to be completed by April 2017. That was relatively simple to do. The maintenance of status is another thing.

Imagine trying to juggle all this reporting without an IT system:
- the date an existing employee was enrolled
- the date someone new starts
- the date a worker turns 22 if this occurs after enrolment
- the date of a worker's 16th birthday when this occurs after the
- enrolment date
- the date birthdates affect retirement (different depending upon your Date of Birth due to changing regulations and 'grandfather clauses')
- the date of any opt-in or opt-out
- deferral date in the case of postponement of enrolment
- assessment dates for all those not considered to be currently an eligible worker to prove their status

...and a whole complex of dates associated with transitional periods and hybrid schemes.

In all your IT decisions use the same creativity and common sense that got you this far with your fast growth business.

Just don't take other people's judgement at face value without thinking through things yourself - preferably with your senior management team -especially if they are IT folk themselves - and so are you!

Holding back technology to preserve broken business models is like allowing blacksmiths to veto the internal combustion engine in order to protect their horseshoes.

Don Tapscott & Anthony D Williams[23]

---

[23] Authors of 'Wikinomics': How Mass Collaboration Changes Everything.

Chapter Five

Roll Call: The people you already have

When you're in a start-up, the first ten people
will determine whether the company succeeds or not.
Each is ten percent of the company.
A small company depends on great people
much more than a big company does.

Steve Jobs

Describe the jobs that you already have
Support staff
- How many?
- Ratio of admin to technical?
- Ratio of managers to the company as a whole and to each team within it.
- If contractors – ratio of contractors to permanent staff
- Ratio of long service vs. newbies

Work ethic
- Do they buck in and do what is needed as they see it?
- Wait to be instructed?
- Work strictly the hours assigned?
- Flexitime?
- Is their work ethic whatever it takes, and then take compensatory time when the rush is off? Do you allow this? How is it monitored? Good judgement with informal checks?

Membership in your marketing without advertising team
- Do they understand the products/services you produce?
- Could they explain what the company does and what makes it different?
- Would they know a potential customer if they met one? If they did how could they engage with them?
- Do they understand the Strategy? I mean in real terms, not as a static document: Who are you and why?

- Are they empowered to make decisions to prevent customer dissatisfaction? Up to what value and within what operational confines? What can they promise, and what not?
- What would they do if they were the only person on site when an important client called with a serious problem?
- Would they recognise that it was an important client? Or a serious problem for that matter.

Putting on a good face
- Who answers the phones? Everyone? Anyone?
- How was the Receptionist trained? How long was the training and what did it consist of?
- Who relieves the receptionist?

How things are done around here – the big stuff
- Do you have an Operations Manual?
- If so, does everyone follow the systems outlined?
- If not, why not?
- Who does the manual updates? How are they handled?

How things are done around here – the small stuff
- Who trains the staff? How? When?
  - o Before they start doing the job?
  - o On the job? As needed?
  - o How do temps learn their functions?

Management
Adapt for a virtual environment

- How many positions?
- How many departments?
- Are they addressed by title? eg. Professor Platypus
- Or by first name?
- Individual offices?
- Personal Assistants of their own?
- Work a lot from home?
- Do they know the Cleaning Person's name? Receptionist? Do You?
- Do they know the names of the Security Guards? Do you?
- Who makes their coffee or tea at work?
- How computer literate?

- Do they change light bulbs, carry in the new supplies if no-one else is there to do it when they are delivered, buy and bring the milk, the flowers on the front desk, clean up their own mess in the refreshment areas?
- Can they explain the order system to anyone?
- Can they place an order themselves, or does their assistant do it? Should they be able to? Or should someone who knows the system do so?
- If you asked, how would they describe the company?
- Would everyone use the same terms?
- Do you think you would all be describing the same company?
- What 3 things about the company's competitive edge would each see as the most important? List these separately per individual.
- What is the best thing about each member of the Management Team? List these separately per individual and tell them.

If you are going to be Shrapnel Free, how your management acts and what they say, both in words and actions, will be critical.

In the sort of growth you are about to experience there are a few important rules:

Rule Number 1.
Everyone IN the company
is potentially a salesman FOR the company

This includes the Security Guard and the Cleaner, all your employees, the kids of your employees, their spouses - but most importantly every member of the Management Team.

If management can't explain the uniqueness of the company and its approach, its product and/or service and make it sound as if it really is worthwhile do something about it: now. Let's suggest a new way to do so.

Acting on the results

The Elevator Pitch - that 30 second grab we have been taught to prepare to describe what our company does.

An Elevator Pitch is the short description of what your company does that you should be able to make in the time you travel down in an elevator with someone who knows nothing about your company.

First do a bit of a test to get the Elevator Pitch of your Management Team members: Get them all together and ask each Manager to write out one sentence that describes the company. Then gather them up and read them out.

Scary huh? You're all obviously working for different companies.

If management can't describe the company memorably, how can anyone else?

All staff should to be able to describe the company easily.

Your senior team should all have the ability to describe why your company is special.

Now here's a radical suggestion: Don't have an 'Elevator Pitch.

Don't thank me for this. I was inspired by an article in LinkedIn by Sam Horn[24].

For years it has been a company strategy mantra that you should have one and make it short and snappy - and memorable of course!

But as Sam pointed out, in her article the problem with an Elevator Speech is that it is, a speech.

You want to engage someone?

Try dialogue.

So, work out together how what your company does makes a difference. Then try to relate it to something with which most people are familiar enough to have an instant connection to it.

The objective is to get your audience to make a mental association that has already been imprinted positively in the common consciousness, and give it your own added value.

Find a way to create a mental bookmark using something with which they are already familiar.

In that way you will keep on reminding the listener about your specialty.

This alternative to the Elevator Pitch is a good way for your whole team to relate to what you do too - and your unpaid marketing team as well.

---

[24] Sam Horn Founder and CEO at The Intrigue Agency, Oct 7, 2015 Why to NEVER Give an Elevator Speech & What to Say Instead. Sam's blogs always add value: www.samhorn.com

Like all good sales tools how you describe your company doesn't focus on the features of your services or products but instead on their benefits to your potential client.

Rowing harder doesn't help
if the boat is headed in the wrong direction.

Kenichi Ohmae[25]

---

[25] www.www.economist.com/node/14031208 Kenichi Ohmae was trained as a nuclear scientist but is best known for his thinking about strategy and for giving insight on the background of those who built great global Japanese companies who were not of any business school but instead used practical experience, vision, and intuition to build their empires. In 1995 Ohmae published 'The End of the Nation State'.

Chapter Six

The extra mile and your team: Can do!

But do you?

*I hire people brighter than me
and I get out of their way.*

Lee Iacocca[26]

People skills

Why should your team, and you, know the names of the Cleaner and the Security Guards?

Well, quite apart from the fact that they're individuals trying to make a living just the same as the rest of you and deserve to be respected as such and not as faceless people, it's good business.

I don't mean just saying Good Morning.

I mean actually talking to them enough that you know who they are as individuals.

Why?

Because courtesy and respect have a way of coming back to you. You're in a fast growth company where all sorts of unexpected things are going to happen.

The Security Guards can go out of their way for one of your customers arriving well after hours with a problem, and win you a name.

Security Guards are in a position to alert you to the small nuances that you may not notice. They can 'own' the company with you and the price on that can be beyond gold.

The same goes for the cleaners.

The cleaners see a lot and hear a lot.

They also clean.

Sounds obvious. Duh!

---

[26] Lee Iacocca worked his way up in Ford as an engineering graduate, moving into sales before becoming a VP and Divisional Manager. His style clashed with that of Henry Ford II, who fired him. Iacocca later became a legendary business leader when he led an almost bankrupt Chrysler Corporation to record profits in the 1980s, leaving it in 1992.

But think about it. They empty rubbish bins, and see what is being thrown out. They see what is on desks.

They work out of normal hours, when the usual buzz of the office is quiet, when staff are relaxed and speak their minds.

They see things objectively as they have no knowledge of the company itself and have no vested interest in its outcome.

They see interactions and hear people mouthing off over tensions and personalities.

They can be an early warning system of the fact that the troops are getting restless.

You may not even know the problems you, as management, have caused in your efforts to build the company while also doing your own jobs. But your cleaners can put two and two together and see that the total is about to rather explosively be more than the expected four!

They can keep that knowledge to themselves and be amused by the predictable fireworks as the shrapnel hits - or kindly alert you that the natives are getting restless so you can do something about it in time.

Also, your cleaners can do an OK job or a good job. If they know you have a big event, they can pull out all the stops – or not.

Who makes the coffee?

Fits the light bulbs when they need replacing?

Fixes the photocopier when it jams?

If management doesn't buck in with the rest of the troops, you're not going to be Shrapnel Free. When things start happening fast and everyone is carrying an individual job responsibility plus those of the people you need but haven't hired yet, watching management treat itself as a rare species will be less than popular.

Why should everyone else make such an effort if the management team doesn't?

Similarly, just as with everyone else in the company, management needs to know the key details about the company.

That doesn't mean that they should try and control things by insisting upon their approval of things that can quite easily happen without them watching every detail. But they should be capable of placing an order in case they are on their own on a weekend or out of hours, when a big order is placed directly with them by top management of a client company and it needs to be rushed through. After all, we are talking here about companies exploding in growth and these things happen.

Or is this sort of immediacy going to risk compromising the effectiveness of the processes there to do the job?

Is there a 'holding pattern' into which the manager can direct the details of the transaction so that it can be rapidly dealt with by the person assigned order entry responsibility?

Should there be?

As a manager you may think you know the process.
You probably don't.

The processes will have been tailored to respond to changing needs and therefore will usually be different from what it once was - and this was done on a 'Needs to Know' basis - and probably you don't need to know.

But you should respect that there are processes in place that others do know – and you being helpful can prove to be quite the opposite.

It's therefore wise to put things into a holding pattern until those who know how best to handle the situation can do so.

Your solution may be inadequate, incorrect, or cause delays or mistakes...best not complicate things in being helpful unless it is absolutely necessary.

Which begs another question: have your group or department heads each drafted a holding pattern for each of their key processes - and made it widely visible and understood? Good idea if they do!

If you design a company where people consider themselves part-owners and want to contribute to the outcome, then you should also design in the fail-safe mechanisms that will stop a well-meaning person from upsetting a carefully arranged process or series of processes or sequences without which the whole thing throws a wobbler.

What can go wrong if someone not familiar with some part of the operation 'bucks in' and causes everyone else to wish they had 'bucked off ' by doing things incorrectly and causing more work than if they had never touched the thing?

State what can, and cannot be tampered with.

Any time someone unfamiliar is engaged in some aspect of the company's operation, be sure that the regular person has a chance to check and verify all is accurate **before** things get acted upon.

Leadership vs. Management

The task of the Directors and Management is difficult in explosive growth.

Directors and managers must steer, but they will also be occasionally required to row in order to stop the ship being sucked over the rapids.

When the company started, everyone rowed. The trick for managers in explosive growth is to know when to stop rowing and let the rowers get on with it (and they probably have rowed once or twice before, so don't need stroke by stroke instruction or supervision, either!).As a member of the senior team (whatever that is called – the team that makes the decisions about the company which will direct its future) your primary job – individually and collectively – is to lead.

You manage things.

You lead people.

It is possible to do both and some leaders are great managers. Few managers are great leaders.

The fallacy that you cannot learn to lead has been often proven to be just that: a fallacy.

Putting someone into a managerial role doesn't immediately give them the tools to do the job.

Most of us are reasonable teachers – we teach our friends new skills, we teach our children how to ride a bike, we teach ourselves when it's a good idea not to say the first thing that comes to mind.

But would any of us approach a classroom of thirty children to teach a subject without some sort of more formal teaching education?

Why is it then unreasonable to expect that a person who wasn't a manager yesterday suddenly becomes one by adding that title?

At best you may be creating what in England is called 'A Jobsworth'. This is someone who upholds petty rules – or even invents them – at the expense of common sense. This is often done because they think that slapping people over the knuckles is a good way of diverting attention from the fact that they have no idea about how to go about the job of managing.

At worst you create the environment where all your hard work of selecting the right people and developing a happy work environment is turned malignant by a festival of spite and backstabbing of some vigour and not a little destruction.

Be aware of the difference between leaders and managers.

*Make sure you haven't inadvertently turned into the sort of manager
you hated working for
because they were so wrapped up in other things
they didn't see or care about the impacts
of their own attitudes, actions and policies.*

What are the three things each of your management team see as important? According to you, or to them?

Try both and see if they match.

If not, then you need to do some listening.

What is the best thing about each member of the Management Team? Write it down, and say why it's important. Ask each manager to do the same for each member of the eta that leads your company. Combine all the comments for each individual as separate lists. Give a copy of the pertinent list to each person.

We all need encouragement. When a company is fast growing a great deal of the time we act instinctively. That takes a lot of confidence – and we all make mistakes. Often we make them because we don't have all the necessary information before we must decide.

Varying levels of success from these decisions can attack our self-confidence. Returning confidence by reading our good points as seen by our peers can be a real boost. And that brings us to:

Rule Number 2:

It is an unwritten law of ratios that the more things
a person does, the more mistakes are likely to be made
by that person, *therefore:*

The person making the most mistakes may not be
the biggest dolt, but instead the highest achiever

Thomas Watson and his son Tom Watson Jnr. (the founding fathers of IBM), Thomas Edison, Bill Fisher of Fisher Controls before its sale to Monsanto, and William McKnight at 3M (who rose from book-keeper to Chairman), were all famous for the way that they mingled with their staff.

They were genuinely interested in people as individuals and remembered names and details about the lives of their employees.

After 30 years of working for Edison, one worker is reported to have said that he never felt as if he was a machinery worker: he was part of a team inventing things.

A long-time worker at Fisher Controls once told me that Bill Fisher always stopped to ask about his children and how their dreams were evolving. It wasn't just to him – it was something Mr. Fisher was known for – and highly respected because of it.

These are qualities worth emulating.

If you are rubbish at remembering details - or even names - get someone who is to be your briefing agent. This has often been my role in supporting senior Directors and Chairmen (some of whom were women) and it has been worthwhile for us all.

As one of my CEOs said: Every company needs an Auntie. An 'Auntie' might be an Uncle. It's someone at the top who shows that they actually care about the people who work there. They show this by listening, by being genuinely interested and actually caring about each individual and his or her triumphs and tragedies.

It doesn't have to be you, but your 'Auntie' or 'Uncle' needs to have your ear. Otherwise you'll never know the richness of personality and style, of sense of humour and of personal toughness and courage represented in your workforce.

You also won't hear their suggestions - and one of those might be the real 'Aha!' moment of your company's future growth.

Make space for creativity

The Minnesota Mining & Manufacturing company 3M has a global footprint and for years it has been a good role model in many ways. We've talked about its brand. However, the battles about alleged cover-ups of possible contamination - with circumstantial evidence of apparent clusters of childhood cancers around 3M plants, suggest that the lessons of how to deal with when things go wrong can well be learned and employed.

As a business leader you are always open to the effects from your business that at the time seemed harmless. History is full of such things. How you deal with real disaster that seems to be of your own making does have legal implications – naturally people don't want to admit liability without being sure of their position. But there are times when that may in fact be not only the right thing to do but the cheapest too. Goliath using his cannons to strike down the little person who is armed only with a slingshot might reverse the myth – but it can also damage your company terminally – and cause you high personal costs – and I don't mean just money.

The good examples from 3M have been much reported and we can learn from them and from the structure they have that has bred innovation over decades.

In fact, 3M was founded on failure. Initially the company was formed to mine Corundum to be used on grinding wheels. Corundum proved to be substandard for the intended use - but from its failure came Wet n Dry sandpaper.

They now cleverly use this analogy in their marketing:

'3M has evolved from mining for rocks to rocking innovation.'

This culture of innovation continues in products that still revolutionise industry today - and the range of industry being influence by 3M innovation is continually growing in diversity.

For over 20 years 3M maintained a leadership position through the power of enabling the innovative thinking of its people. Now it adds collaboration with others to find solutions to their needs.

The company's 15% thinking rule is thought to have inspired that at Google of 20%. Officially, each person has to spend 15% of work time in what they call Intellectual Doodling. This evolved from William McKnight when he became General Manager in 1914. He started the philosophy of 'Listen to anybody with an idea'. He also memorably stated that management's biggest mistake is to tell someone in authority how to do their job.

In EDS Germany before it was sold to HP, my manager Vassilios Vlachos (now VP NTT Data Germany) enabled and encouraged this 'intellectual doodling' within his team and factored it into our budget. We still achieved over $30K above target per person in a 300 person team - so saying you can't afford it just means you didn't plan for it.

Out of this intellectual doodling Eugen Oetringer, at the time a Systems Architect, wrote a thoughtful analysis of IT Strategy Management[27] as well as a ground-breaking book about Autism being like congestion on the data highways of computer networks.

Oetringer's books were well based from research that led to him holding several patents in devices for use in the management of neural networks[28].

---

[27] The IT Strategy Management Process: Supporting IT Services Through Effective Knowledge Management Eugen Oetringer ISBN 10: 9077212264 / ISBN 13:9789077212264

[28] Surprise Treatment for Dyslexia, ADHD, Headaches and Other Conditions - It's All About Information Management Eugen Oetringer ISBN: 9781412095860

These books generated fresh interest and also brought new and otherwise unidentified clients. His success reflected well on our group.

Intellectual doodling can also be called by other names. Cal Newport, in an excellent thought-provoking book of the name[29], calls it Deep Work.

Here is his definition:

Deep Work:

"Professional activities performed in a state of distraction-free concentration that push your cognitive capabilities to their limit. These efforts create new value, improve your skill, and are hard to replicate."

It seems that scientific studies of our capacity for concentration demonstrate our propensity to be lured into undemanding Shallow Work. These are the things that are often performed while being distracted. They create no new value.

The tenet of his book is that Deep Work needs fostering now more than ever, as the internet age offers Shallow Work in abundance and with alluring enticement.

The companies that embrace the need for periods of concentrated work in isolation from distraction - like 3M and others - reap the benefits of Deep Work's productive and creative outcomes.

Newport cites the example of software company, Basecamp[30] (then called 37Signals) that took radical steps to foster Deep Work. To encourage it, they reduced their work week to four days. That doesn't mean cramming five days of work into four days.

Co-founder Jason Fried explained in a Blog that this shorter week forced elimination of the time wasting activities that for most workers fill out a significant amount of a five day work week. According to the book, following the success of this strategy, the company now shuts down for the whole month of June so people can work on their own projects. At the 'Show and Tell' that follows the June thinking period, the resulting ideas, new products, business opportunities and developments are showcased and voted upon - the winners being developed further.

---

[29] Deep Work: Cal Newport ISBN-10: 1455586692

[30] www.basecamp.com/about Basecamp/37Signals Basecamp, now re-named 37Signals is a web-based project management tool.37Signals, the company, also created Ruby on Rails

Newport points out that many technology companies like Google allot 20% of work time to individuals working on self-generated projects. Has this generated a profitable company for Bootcamp?

From the book 'REWORK' based on growing 37Signals and written by co-founders Jason Fried and David Heinemeyer Hansson, these points stand out:

- Minimise mass – in everything (in other words stay small and uncomplicated): more mass needs more management.
- Make a decision: you can always change it later.
- Focus on what won't change, not what's fashionable
- Sell your by-products: something that at Archer we work with our clients to identify and do.
- Break things into small chunks. Estimates are usually out – be out by smaller bits on smaller chunks, not by a lot on a big project.
- Make big plans one tiny decision at a time.
- Let customers outgrow you instead of trying to be all things to them.
- Marketing is not a department.

Fried recounts the company's dance with Venture Capital (VC) firms and other would-be investors. The dance proved too tiresome and potentially destructive to their goals, so they didn't respond to these investors. Their reason for not doing so was that they want to deliver what their customers want - not what investors want.

However, when Jeff Bezos sent an email via his personal secretary, this was something different. Eventually Bezos invested in Basecamp. What this gave the company was a hedge against risk and what Fried describes as "access to the brain of one of today's greatest living entrepreneurs."

Perhaps when you race towards the VC Dance Hall you may think through what you really want for your company and whether any of your potential dance partners suit your style.

In this case it's not considered bad etiquette to seek out a dance partner who does - and one from whom you can benefit beyond money: through their influence, provocative thoughts, experience, and guidance. You don't **have** to dance to someone else's tune.

Consider the most successful top privately held companies whose names you probably know:

- Aldi - the supermarket chain that also is the parent company of Trader Joe's
- Bosch - automotive, industrial and household machinery
- PricewaterhouseCoopers, Deloitte, Ernst & Young, and KPMG - the 'Big Four' accounting and consulting firms

- Mars and Ferrero (Ferrero Rocher) - the confectioners
- Bechtel the global engineering and construction (E&C) giant
- Cargill –the agricultural food and fertiliser company
- The John Lewis Partnership in UK, El Cortes Ingles in Spain, E. Leclerc in France - department stores
- IKEA
- Chanel
- Red Bull
- Lego

*If well respected companies can build global success
without shareholders, perhaps you can too.*

Salutary thoughts as you grow.

The example of Basecamp is not meant for you to follow. It is meant to cause you to think, and to be as creative as what got you this far already when you are planning the future of your company and how it will operate, be structured, and act.

We are guiding you in the lashing of your Bamboo Scaffolding so that it will enable better insight into the inner workings of your company now and in the future.

By way of comparison to Basecamp consider another example from Newport's book.

In 2013, as the new CEO of Yahoo, former early Google employee and consequently one of the largest shareholders in Google, Marissa Mayer took a different stance on time to think.

Having checked the server logs to assess activity of those not working in the office, Mayer banned all working from home. Because people were not constantly interacting by email or other communication tools, her verdict was that unless she could see and measure activity in this way, they were not working - and said as much.

Mayer's measure of successful output was activity, not results.

Was Yahoo a success under this leadership? According to the value of the company now, versus when Mayer took the senior role, no.

Has it been successful for Mayer? So it would seem. Pending shareholders approval, at the time of writing Verizon had just bought Yahoo in April 2017. Mayer is reported to receive an estimated$186m, having been paid $200million over the previous five years. Her staying on is not part of the deal, according to a Guardian article by Dominic Rushe[31].

Rushe goes on to say that her payout is not as much as it could have been. According to that article Mayer will lose her 2017 bonus of around $2million because of the breach of Yahoo's security in 2014.

This was when Yahoo reported that 26 account holders had their details hacked. It transpired later that the real number was considerably greater -allegedly around 500 million.

Not all of us can sit at the Corporate Round Table. In the book 'Corpocracy'[32] published in 2008, Robert A. G. Monks gives some insight into how failure as a CEO of a global corporation can be so rewarding.

Not all Mayer's decisions were of this calibre and many employees found her approachability refreshing and inspiring. She responded to emails from employees who were way down the totem pole and to many of her staff this meant a lot.

Cathy Lesjak, the Chief Financial Officer of HP in her role as Interim CEO also made personal email responses to staff at every level. She publically stated she would not stand for the permanent role. Many wished she had.

At Yahoo, Mayer's strategy to build talent through acquisition may yet prove sound in the long term, but an article listing the fate of the companies acquired under her period as CEO[33] suggests that bringing talent to a company devoid of innovation is only half of an equation for success. Deep Work fosters that environment.

*As you plan for the success
of your own fast growth company*

*I guess the question really comes down to
whether you are there to create something you are proud of, and that
adds value to the world we all share.*

---

[31] www.theguardian.com/technology/2017/apr/25/yahoo-marissa-mayer-payout-186-million

[32] Corpocracy: How CEOs and the Business Roundtable Hijacked the World's Greatest Wealth Machine... And How to Get It Back' ISBN-10: 047014509952

[33] https://gizmodo.com/heres-what-happened-to-all-of-marissa-mayers-yahoo-acqu-1781980352

In short, is your focus based on the things that never go out of style: good customer service, reliability, effectiveness, smart solutions, giving back, having fun, being professional?

Do you base your business on enduring values: tell the truth; make a difference; treat people well?

If you do, your investment of creativity, time and commitment creates value beyond the material wealth you deserve for creating a company of worth.

Whether you do is a question for you, not me.

It is a question whose answer will influence the decisions you make and the teams you build . It is one worth thinking about.

How do you keep your best technical people?

3M operates a dual career ladders for technical specialists so that they can rise on an equal footing of influence and financial reward as managers. This means the company keeps good technicians and scientists – and doesn't end up with good technical people who are poor managers.

What sort of rewards should innovation bring?

A staff member inventing a new product, service or market for 3M will be the head of that business - at the highest ranking, and with the commensurate salary and benefits as any other general Manager, Vice President or Divisional Leader.

There are many ways to reward innovative success and yours should suit your company and be fair to both the originator and the company.

Managing Failure

We mentioned briefly the implications of a steady hand and authenticity of response when things go wrong – and the costs that may be attached.

Two thoughts worth considering about failure:

Edison famously said:

I have not failed.
I've just found 10,000 ways that won't work.

Just because something doesn't do
what you planned it to do doesn't mean it's useless.

Founder of IBM, Thomas Watson Snr., was asked if he was going to fire someone whose decision had just cost IBM $600,000. Watson's view was that he had just given the person a $600,000 training course. Why fire him and let someone else benefit from that experience?

Failure is part of the culture of innovative companies.

Managing failure doesn't mean rewarding negligence. It means that managers become more involved.

A failure-tolerant manager can distinguish between excusable and inexcusable mistakes because of being sufficiently involved to identify the elements of the whole process and also being approachable enough to get the real story.

This culture encourages the pursuit of thoughtfully developed projects. These usually produce productive results, even if they fail. It is often these failures that give insight into what works.

Rethink how your company deals with failure.
It's worth factoring it into the plan.

Valuing your temps and contract workers
Remember Rule Number 1?

Rule Number 1.
Everyone IN the company
is potentially a salesman FOR the company

So shouldn't everyone be able to describe what the company does? Well yes, as we have already discussed. But with your staff you need to work upwards towards this and not the other way around. They need to be able to really grasp the essence, if not the detail, about what it is that makes the company's products and services so special, not just recite a trite sentence without understanding what it summarises.

Why bother with making sure a temporary worker knows all this? Isn't that eating into the time you are paying at a high rate for their relief work?

Why does your temp typist/warehouse worker/packer need to know all that?

Because we don't know who he or she is married to, who his or her Dad or Mother may be, or for that matter, who he/she is. Many people use temp work to put some bread and butter on the table in between jobs - while they are writing a book (I did!) - or developing the latest scientific whatnot for the goozywinder (that might make them market dominant in their field in the future) - and tomorrow they can be the person with the power to influence the future of your company.

As a Temp I have worked beside one of the few Satellite Receiving Station technicians in the world - between contracts and saving for a new house; a former central government specialist in sporting infrastructure – made redundant and seeking the next permanent gig; a highly skilled research chemist with a PhD - new to the country and seeking a permanent role to carry on his earlier work in detecting markers for cancer drugs.

Don't discount your occasional workers as being low-skilled or unemployable as permanent staff.

That's where your Company Aunt or Uncle comes in.

Your temps may be the your best recruiting ground.

It may be that your Temp talks to a Venture Capitalist about what a great company it is.

It may be that she talks to the biggest client in the market - the person you can never get to return a call. It may be that his daughter, Juanita, is a key purchasing officer, the industry's most respected journalist, or whatever.

Who knows how the influence may spin?

Don't presume that the people who are on your staff, even temporarily, don't have networks potentially influential to your future.

I worked as a temp for a private health insurance company called Medicash that was honourable. It is not an adjective commonly used in describing an insurance company.

Later, not as a temp, I have found one similar in the not-for-profit company Western Provident Association (WPA), another British Medical Insurer. State Farm in the USA shares the same qualities.

Medicash is based in Liverpool, England, and actually use good common business sense and kindness in dealing with their customers - even allowing for small print. Where common sense showed a reason to do so, the agents responded accordingly in their claim handling.

As a temp with Medicash I saw this first hand and I have related that story countless times to many different potential customers – and did become a customer myself.

When a customer asks the temp or contract worker a question about what the company does, do you want the answer to be: "I really haven't a clue. I'm just a temp"?

An unknown good plan is useless

As I mentioned, part of my objectives in my first management role was to stem a 45% staff turnover. The company had two main divisions. People in each had no idea what the other did, what products they sold, who their clients were – yet they shared all the same support systems and the same Order Processing staff.

They all worked for the same company but thought they worked for the Division.

One day I saw something that epitomised the whole fiasco. The senior managers of each of the two divisions were in the centre of an open plan office – one at each end of a padded modular partition – each proclaiming ownership.

I walked up to them and said quietly: "Gentlemen. The children are watching! May I help by making a third claim until we can resolve this issue elsewhere?"

On another occasion an agitated administrative assistant appeared in the opening to my own cubicle. She had been told that all of the fonts and layouts of standard templates for one division had to be done in a font quite different from the standard.

One of her colleagues had the perfect solution. It was ingenious: "That's easy", she said. "Everyone else's standards can match!" Hey presto. The moment passed without the impact it was desired to achieve.

The place was like a hive of very cross bees. Small feudal wars were everywhere.

It started at reception. Can you imagine? The receptionist didn't even know what products were made by the company, or who the key clients were. And she was the one who was the first point of contact.

But maybe you can imagine! Does yours?

It wasn't until I held a workshop entitled "Contrary to popular belief there IS a system" that they had any clue about what a brilliant range of products were sold - or that the principle client for one division was the Space Program.

They truly didn't believe that there was a system in place - let alone understood how it worked. Sound familiar?

How did they find out? I had each division's sales team do a sales presentation to the other division on their range of products. It was fascinating to watch the responses.

People were impressed and that look of 'Wow. I didn't know that' was well worth the effort of holding the event.

Then I did a presentation based around a simple one page flow chart that showed how the order processing system worked, explaining what caused delays, how they could be fixed, and who had control over the timing of specific types of delays.

People toddled off with their one page maps of the system muttering to themselves that they didn't know it was NASA holding things up waiting approval on testing... or the Federal Government doing due diligence... or...They even apologised for giving the Order Processing staff unearned grief.

Suddenly they all worked for the same company, one of which they were even more proud of than when they defensively worked for one of its Divisions.

The point about each of these examples is that if you think to the root cause of the issue, the solution is often a lot simpler than you thought at your first pass at trying to find one.

The most serious mistakes are not being made

as a result of wrong answers.

The truly dangerous thing is asking the wrong questions.

Peter Drucker[34] - Men, Ideas & Politics

First impressions

Let's go back to the receptionist and the phone answering.

Perhaps your system has been that whoever is nearest answers the phone and hands it across the desk to the relevant person.

As you grow this is no longer practical.

You need to think about the importance of the receptionist.

If you are a Virtual Company are you going to be truly virtual or are you going to capitalise on the personality of your people?

How? What will your virtual equivalent of a receptionist be? Remember Rule Number 1?

Rule Number 1.
Everyone IN the company
is potentially a salesman FOR the company.

No one more so than the all-important first point of contact.

---

[34] Peter Drucker was the first to realise that management was a distinct function. His 39 books and many articles adapted to the impacts of the times and he was prepared to rethink or argue against his own earlier thoughts.

*Know what your customers want most
and what your company does best.
Focus on where those two meet.*

Kevin Stirtz[35]

Does your receptionist know what the company sells? Why it is so good? Is he excited about it? He should be. If he isn't, someone needs to explain it so he is.

He? Equal opportunity - or not? One of the companies for which I worked had a major trauma when we wanted to hire a male receptionist. Talk about reverse discrimination. You?

In our one day Professional Learning Course 'The Reflective Receptionist' we tailor a short front of house overview to educate everyone who answers the main switchboard. Your key front-of-house staff, receptionists and anyone who relieves them (including a temp) should have the same sort of training. If you haven't the time to do so from within your team, get someone externally to plan and deliver this for you – but review the content beforehand. This will require you and your team to give a proper briefing to the course designer.

The objective is that everyone who answers the phone understands and has the ability to do this.

In our course we include knowledge of the company products and services and spell out your market differentiation. We explain some of the problems of explosive growth so your receptionist can catch the shrapnel before it penetrates to the troops who are, after all, particularly vulnerable. They have their noses down and bottoms up busily building your successful company. They certainly won't appreciate shrapnel in their exposed parts!

A good receptionist can even get the warring factions to lower their rifles.

After the introduction to Front-of-House, with whomever you arrange it the Receptionist(s) will also know:
- key clients – by company and by individual name
- key corporate calendar dates
- managers names, how the company is structured, and why

---

[35] Kevin Stirtz describes himself as a Change Maker, connecting data, strategy and people. He works for Thomson Reuters Analytics Strategy Team and is based in Eagan, Minnesota just south of St. Paul alongside the Mississippi River and his team works out the data you need for decision-making and enabling growth.

There are a lot of other details that need to be covered so no matter who answers your 'phones or greets your customers or visitors in person, they are well equipped to shine and show the company in its best light.

There is coaching on challenging questions, so that the people who answer your phones and greet your customers are always well armed to handle Rule Number One. No one can be expected to know all the answers but everyone should have some well-designed holding patterns into which to steer problematic queries or situations until they can be dealt with by the person who can address them well.

Other staffing issues - who sits where on the bus

Get the right people on the bus –
and the wrong people off the bus.

Jim Collins - Good to be Great[36]

The founder of 3Pillar Global, David deWolf, writes an interesting article[37] about this quote. It's based on his own experience of growing a fast growth company. In it, he points out that this is all very well, but should be set against the reality that it's not easy when you get the right people on the bus to get them into the right seats – and even harder to get the wrong people off the bus.

Who needs to get off?

He points out that you can, and often need to put up with some levels of less than ideal behaviour from high performers, but even they can exceed everyone's capacity to deal with the aggravation. When they do, even they need to get off the bus.

I once hired someone on a short term contract to assist me in managing an exceedingly heavy workload. My diary was a headache to coordinate. There were no overlaps possible or the whole day would be chaos for me and everyone concerned. I was interviewing up to eight people a day and doing my own job as well. I needed a Traffic Director.

Handing over control of the diary meant I did nothing without consulting this new Traffic Director first – even going out for lunch. It worked fantastically well. I had an exceptionally competent Traffic Director and things ran smoothly – but just for me.

---

[36] Jim Collins is a Stanford MBA, ex-McKinsey and HP is an author and student of company growth and sustainability, author and management teacher..

[37] David deWolf established 3Pillar Global in 2006. They are now a leader in developing software that helps client build product growth . www.daviddewolf.com/its-not-about-getting-the-right-people-on-the-bus.

My excellent Traffic Director was upsetting the rest of my team so much that they were all walking on eggshells and tempers were fraying.

It was a classic case of the cat amongst the pigeons and the bus ride had to end.

When the Directors asked why, my response was that I could have one high performer and no team – or a good performing team, so there was no choice.

In cases like this, deWolf gives the following good advice:

Be deliberate, decisive, and move on.

You might just need someone to change seats. deWolf goes on to caution that you can't ask someone to change seats without telling them where to sit. His advice is:

Develop a plan, define clear success criteria, and persevere.

Ambiguity when moving seats is a disaster.

He also points out that you might find there are a quite a few people who need to get off the bus – and that might mean reupholstering the seats.

In other words, a complete change of organisational structure might be the real requirement.

Wrong bus or wrong seat?

What about the person who was the perfect person when you were just a few people gathered around three desks and passing the phone to each other, but is now obviously not coping with the changes?

This is one of the most common and one of the hardest of the challenges you will face. A person may have been with you from the start. He, or she, may have been loyal and true. But lately as the needs of the job have changed beyond recognition, this same person is quite dreadfully out of his or her depth.

Do you say: "Thanks, but we don't need you anymore?" Hardly. But how do you handle this most common scenario?

You have to decide if there is a space for that person in the new structure, or not. Is there something that can be done by this person using the skill levels of the past that will still pay their way in your lean and growing company?

Don't just think this through yourself. How about involving him or her in the solution? You may be surprised to find that the person is fully aware of personal limitations and fears losing the job.

Perhaps he or she has already thought of a possible solution: perhaps if not, he or she would put some effort into finding one if you revealed your willingness to work it out.

The hard reality is that in explosive growth everyone needs to be a contributing party to the whole. Everyone will be carrying quite enough load without also doing the work of someone who is getting paid to carry their own, and not keeping up. The bus has only so many seats at any given time and each seat holder has to contribute to the whole.

How many activities make a job?

In every company a mountain of tasks exists that together could form a job. Is this an option?

Is there another job coming up which will have a limited focus and specific deadlines with which the person could cope?

What are the 'part' jobs that people don't have time to do, but squeeze in any way when they can and in short time slots not suited to the fact that they're not familiar enough with the task, or interested enough in it, to do it rapidly and well? The things like:

- ordering supplies
- moving files to secure storage
- handling all the details for meetings
- being the first point of contact for customer queries so only the complex things get through to technical people but the simple or generic things are immediately answered
- booking flights on the internet (very time consuming but perhaps already outsourced)
- doing information searches or research on the internet
- short reports on competitive advantage/status
- identifying and documenting market trends
- undertaking the induction training
- training the reception team
- handling all interview correspondence
- tracking the mail in and out - you do have a system to do that don't you? If not, you should.
- Warehousing and distribution
- Powerpoint presentations. (If you use Powerpoint)
- putting together all the generic information needed for proposals
- maintaining a literature library including all company documents
- managing the Boiler Plate library of standard texts
- maintaining the meeting kit - that box of essentials you should have ready to go rather than someone haring about grabbing this and that at the last minute and leaving key items behind

- maintaining the Capital Assets Inventory and managing Licence Agreements so they don't expire without due attention (you do have one and do have Licence Agreement details listed somewhere central don't you? And an up-to-date Asset register? You should)
- maintaining all service requirements on equipment, machinery and vehicles
- arranging corporate events

Where is the bus headed?

In an article in the Economist in 2001, Peter Drucker stated that future work will be dominated by the fact that people will want to know what the company is doing and where it is going. Next they want personal responsibility and a sense of achievement.

He has again been proven correct.

That should be your destination too.

The final bus stop for favoured status

Perhaps there is a person who has played on the fact of being here since day one and having a special relationship with you, the Big Boss – or one of the senior management team.

- Is poor performance expected to be acceptable because of this preferred status?
- Is the person making serious errors and demonstrating less than desirable work practices?
- Would you get rid of him or her if you could?

Then you may find it hard to do, but you have very little choice. You can either be a disagreeable person to one individual or to the rest of the company.

Why should everyone else valiantly carry the extra burdens of rapid growth while one person flaunts a preferential status?

Everyone deserves a chance to perform well, but if that has long since gone by, then face the need to address the situation.

Be honest with yourself - or if it's not you who has endowed this status (intentionally or otherwise), but a member of the early Management Team, it's time for a chat.

Gloves off: it cannot go on. Otherwise you will start finding shrapnel-loaded landmines laid by some of your most valued staff.

Getting people off the bus in ways
so that they remain advocates of your company is an art.

However, if you base your actions on deliberate and measured steps, and show genuine care for both your organisation and its future as well as for the future best fit for the person alighting from the bus- you'll find it easier.

A Person's a person,
no matter how small.

Dr. Seuss[38]

---

[38] Dr. Seuss was the pen name of Theodor Seuss Geisel, who actually left Oxford as an undergraduate and only received an honourary Doctorate towards the end of his life. He was a prolific writer and cartoonist and his much loved children's books have sold over 600 million copies.

Chapter Seven

Needles in hay stacks:

Who you need to hire right now.

Hire an attitude, not just experience and qualification.

Greg Savage[39]

It is widely reported that there is a shortage of people with the right skills -especially in IT.

I propose that there is not such a skill deficit.

Instead there is a deficit of elegantly simple ways to identify talent.

In our current way of doing things, seldom does the hiring manager even have a chance to peruse a CV that doesn't have the right key words.

Hiring the right people is the greatest challenge for any company. The methods used today to find the right people are almost by definition not going to identify the talent you need without you supplementing the process.

It used to be that Recruitment Agencies met and interviewed both clients and candidates so they understood pretty well who would fit where to perform best.

Now, except in the case of exceptional recruitment companies, most of this is done by email and by online parsing of resumés and blind contact to a person who's CV just has the right key words.

Add this into the context that now many companies have strict hiring processes that rely on systems like Taleo.

These systems require hiring parameters to fit into pre-existing one-size-fits-all templates. Such a system makes it pretty hard for a big

---

[39] Greg Savage is an Australian trainer of recruitment professionals and companies worldwide and writes a blog on recruitment for a global audience.

company to find someone suitable – but resorting to these same methods for your hybrid mix of talent, drive, and fun that describes your crew is almost guaranteed to be ineffective at best, and disastrous at worst.

It is well worth setting your own hiring practices. If you must automate the process, choose a system that reflects your needs. Check out sites like Capterra[40] to see what is available.

You need to first set out a clear seven point selection check list for each position.

Only seven points? Yes. Only seven.

Most hiring parameters are extensive. They sound so tediously similar and self-serving it is a wonder the right person ever emerges from the process.

Do you really need a degree? In some cases you do. In others, equivalent experience is acceptable - or even better.

Do you really need the person to be highly presentable if they will never see a client in person?

Describe the jobs you need filling right now.

In our one day Professional Learning Course 'FIT: Hire people, not skills' we work with your teams to create templates that will help you describe effectively both the company and the job itself. These have been designed so that a busy staff member can break from work, scan a CV, take these templates and questions and do a sound, credible interview every time. You can do the same. The following process will help you focus.

List all the jobs you need to fill right now

_____

_____

_____

_____

_____

_____

[40] www.capterra.com

_____

_____

_____

- What would happen if you didn't fill each of these?
- What is the pressure to fill them?
- How are you coping now?
- How much longer can you cope like this?
- If you don't find the right person within the required time, how else can you solve the problem?
- Do you have to hire direct employees?
- Can they be contractors?
- If you saw the right person for the company and for future roles you knew you would need but the company was not quite up to that need just yet, what would you do?
- Can the work itself be outsourced or does it **have** to be done in-house?
- Would it be better done through a company or individual who did nothing else but that and therefore could possibly do it in fraction of the time and possibly do it better? Publicity may be one such item.
- If so, how do you ensure that your company ethos is sustained in their delivery of the services or goods they supply on your behalf?
- If you didn't find someone who was really right for the job, could you manage with someone who fitted with the company, if not for that particular role but could probably take off some of the pressure?
- If so, what happens when that job is filled by someone with the right skills and the right fit?

In explosive growth it is not always possible to find the right person at the right time. But if you think you make do with a non-fit, think again. You haven't time to go about mending the scaffolding when the hurricane hits.

Any non-fitting person is going to be as dangerous a piece of shrapnel as you can imagine. He or she can wear through the bonds that are holding things together faster than you would believe.

Don't even go there. Just don't do it! You're better thinking through other solutions than putting someone in a position just because they are breathing.

Outsourcing

You may decide that jobs like payroll, back office work like Customer Enquiries or Help Desk are best done by professional companies.If you are outsourcing what is often called 'back office support' functions we urge you to be very wary and manage this relationship with clearly defined performance objectives based on customer satisfaction, not on length of time per call.

For all sub-contracted service providers make sure that:

- you agree the training content and review the training;
- you monitor activity through Mystery Shopping (agreed always with the client beforehand as a term of engagement and advised to all of their operators so they are aware that they are being monitored) – and check that they actually do that and don't just say they do!
- any fulfilment activities such a company manages on your behalf are effective and that delivery times are reliably within the limits you have agreed, and that they have effective delivery tracking with any of their own outsourced delivery agents.

This might seem obvious but take the now remedied case of the UK's Royal Mail.

Following outsourcing of the Royal Mail post delivery in the early 2000s, reliability and security were quickly compromised when the lowest bidder secured the contract. The new company responsible quickly found that finding good staff was challenging because they had won the contract on fees below market rate.

Other recruitment companies refused to supply their good temp staff at low rates when the successful bidder needed people. As a result, the least educated and often least motivated people were hastily put into the roles.

The staff cuts that followed the outsourcing lost many a friendly postman who knew the route, the people, and the sorts of mail they received - and therefore provided more than a mail delivery service. They alerted authorities when things 'weren't right', saving lives and property damage as well as being efficient and honourable mail deliverers. They served much wider community benefit beyond the excellent job they did of delivering the post.

When temp workers were shuffled from one route to another, sometimes mail bags were emptied into local rubbish tins or post was opened and cash and cheques and credit cards removed. The temporary post people were loaded into taxis to be taken to their routes in areas with which they were unfamiliar, so getting mail to the right address became problematic from what was once one of the most respected and effective mail systems in the world.

It was a disaster of national scale and would have made a great comedy if it hadn't been the Royal Mail, a former benchmark in postal excellence.

We are back to enjoying a friendly, reliable and trustworthy regular post person at last, but experience can be an expensive teacher.

In general, make it a rule that with any outsourced activity you ensure actions are in place to prove that **your** quality standards are met by those acting in your name.

Any company providing service under your brand

should be a good fit with your own culture.

Review all the following elements to have a successful outsourcing relationship:

- your value on customer responsiveness is shared - or bettered
- there is proven capability to provide the service - review track record and check with previous users if you can
- the ability to adapt to any changes in your needs without severe penalties is secure - get case studies
- you have agreed a clear and proven issues resolution process
- an exit from the relationship is not excessively costly

The Crowd as staff

Crowd-sourcing is becoming an important part of enlisting customers as employees. Sometimes they are even free - but usually crowd-sourced helpers gain some sort of recognition or reward for being a part of the design team - or whatever component of the business in which they are engaged.

Lego is a great example. Anyone can submit a design for a new Lego piece. Users vote on the design and if there is sufficient interest, the designer gets a 1% royalty on the net revenue.

Kraft and Dell source product ideas from the Crowd, and Samsung has a complete lab to engage individuals, companies and researchers in idea generation.

Manage expectations.

Input is not decision making.

Contractors and Contracts

While many big outsourcing companies are struggling, there is an explosion in growth in small and highly skilled service companies providing components of what used to be the Organisational Pyramid.

If you get the right partner for this usually they are better at it, cheaper, and more effective, because that aspect of your total business is their total business.

It is worth examining components of what you do now in your current structure to see if this makes sense for you. It may give you a lot more flexibility. Done poorly, it may also give you some shrapnel to dodge – but that is the same with all business decisions.

You may hire a short-term contractor until the right person can be found to join the permanent staff.

If you outsource parts of the company operation, take the time to win over your outsourcing company to the belief that you have a fantastic company serving a unique market niche.

Excite them! Who do they work for apart from you? Many of your potential clients.

Your business collaborators and partners
can also be members of your unpaid sales force.

The right person at the wrong time

What will you do when you find people who fit really well, but you just don't have the job there at the moment? They are ideal for the company. You know there are skills there that you will need in the future.

It happens. Do you let them go or do you grab them while they are in your sights?

If you possibly can, grab them. If they're the right people now, they will probably be the right people later. But if you let them go thinking they will still be around, the chances are that they will be - in a competitive company, not yours.

Find a way to make them productive - even at a break-even level - and get them on the team. If you explain the predicament to the applicants, you may be surprised at the innovative ways suggested to make inclusion on the team quickly remunerative to the company. It may even open up avenues of revenue you hadn't thought about. In explosive growth the right team is everything. If at all possible, get the right people on board, even if it means real penny pinching.

Document these decisions as they happen. All management decisions that could be considered out of the norm should have some sort of documentation: a scribbled note attached to a sheet of reference paper or invoice copy. Then drop this record into the Future Funding folder.

That's the folder you are going to refer to when you need an injection of investment capital or to take out a bigger bank loan. If all you have to do is pull out the file and organise the information into one credible document, it will make your justification case much easier.

You'll be able to demonstrate that there was consideration behind your decisions and in this way show that your success was as much a result of planning and your own sound business philosophy as an accurate sense of the way your business is supplying a much needed response to the market's current needs.

Hiring for fit

PayPal is a great example of creating a team that fits. What they had in common was a passion to create a new form of money.

That is what each of them was hired for - that passion. They hired not for particular credentials, although the obvious talents of the people they chose were a necessary part of the equation.

The critical decision-making factor in hiring was whether they would enjoy working together.

As Peter Thiel says in his book 'Zero to One: Notes on Startups or How to build the future', talented people don't need to work for you. He says that the reason they elect to do so is because you can describe to them that what you are working on that is compelling and important - and that the way you tell them this excites them about the future of your product or service and your company and therefore about their future as well.

If you can't describe why your company is a great personal match to the individual, then it probably isn't.

Thiel says the first few talented people might come for the Stock Options- but focus on why the 20th person wants to work for you.

In PayPal's case before they sold to eBay, their reason was to "do irreplaceable work on a unique problem alongside great people".

You notice the emphasis here is on making yourself attractive to the right people - not on what salaries or benefits you offer. It is taken as given that you will offer fair market value for the skills and talent you hire.

Thiel also emphasises that hiring decisions are too important to outsource. There is no argument from us.

Company culture doesn't exist.
A company is a culture.

It's a tribe and only those with the same tribal preferences
will feel at home.

PayPal is a compelling example of a hiring practice that worked. They say it worked well because they were all the same type of nerd. Nerds they maybe but certainly rather special nerds.

The builders of PayPal are a remarkable group of high achievers who went on to continue building things once PayPal was sold:

- Peter Thiel co-founded Palantir, the big data analysis company revolutionising how US Government departments parse and analyse data
- David Sachs co-founded Yammer, the open source private enterprise social networking solution that enables interdepartmental wikis and communication
- Jeremy Stoppelman and Russell Simmons founded Yelp
- Jawed Karim founded UTube
- Elon Musk founded SpaceX and co-founded Tesla Motors.

They have continued to help each other build success after success. Now THAT is fit.

People magnets – finding the right people

We all know that interviewing is about making the right hiring decisions.

Who you hire reflects on your ability to choose well. It is therefore VITAL that you have accurately decided what sort of qualities and abilities will be best for the job before you start the process.

That is not as easy as it sounds. Most courses, videos, and books on the subject of Selection Interviewing concentrate on the interview itself.

However, unless you get the definition right, you will constantly be caught in the worry cycle with your interviews. That's because unless we do this, we have nothing to back up our judgements, or against which to compare similar candidates

These days you can be audited on those decisions and may need to defend your selection process if legally challenged as to why you selected as you did. Your records need to be impeccable and show a clear decision basis and consistency in measuring candidates against the same criteria.

However, a standard measure is not enough. It must be a measure precisely geared for the job to be done. This makes it important to spend some care and attention in reviewing what ACTUALLY is needed. Don't accept a Job Description from someone without sitting down and having a chat about it.

Make the writer qualify WHY what is claimed to be necessary is in fact, a realistic requirement. If that seems a bit harsh, or like extra work, remember that the object is to find the person who will do the job and do it well despite their paper credentials. Let me give an example from history.

In the 1930s, Miss Gladys Aylward was a parlour maid in England.

Gladys had a burning conviction that she was destined to go to China as a missionary. After much difficulty, she was finally able to secure a place in a training programme.

However, after some time the missionary society rejected her. Gladys had failed theology. She failed most of the subjects they tried to teach her, subjects defined as essential to do the job. In addition, as they pointed out to her in their rejection, by the time Gladys reached China she would be thirty. The Missionary Society had no faith that a person of that age could effectively learn Chinese. For all these reasons, she was therefore considered unfit.

But Gladys was determined to succeed at what she felt called to do. She had a heartfelt understanding of Christianity. It didn't fit into theological boxes; hers was of a more practical sort.

Undaunted by having to proceed to her calling without the official mantle of the Missionary Society, and using her own savings, Gladys set off on a journey that would have discouraged most.

She crossed the Channel by boat-train, continued by train through the Netherlands, Germany, Poland, Russia via Moscow and across Siberia to Vladivostok; by boat to Japan; by train the length of Japan; by boat to China; train to Peking, and then by mule into Tibet - all this in the middle of winter.

Then she had to learn Chinese!

From a very difficult start on her own in the mountains of Tibet, Gladys became fluent in the language, a trusted community leader - and a very successful missionary. Through her influence, the local Mandarin banned the ancient practice of binding the feet of young women, making Gladys his Foot Inspector.

Then the Japanese invaded and due to her defence of the local people she was interrogated by Japanese soldiers who beat her with their rifles. Determined to save her orphanage children from similar actions, there was only one escape - over the mountains on little used trails.

Despite being wounded herself, Gladys walked almost a hundred children to safety away from the invading forces. They had a tiny supply of food when they set out. After a month of incredible hardship they reached safety.

This was the 'Small Woman' about whom the film 'The Inn of the Sixth Happiness' was made. In the film Ingrid Bergman starred as Gladys.

Gladys benefited from the interest generated by the film in assisting funding for her Taiwanese children's home that she later formed, but she was deeply upset by the historical inaccuracies of the film. It trivialised her independent efforts and physical hardships in getting to Tibet, gave a false depiction of the Mandarin Lin Nan as being half European which she thought insulted his long Chinese lineage - and created a fictional romance between them.

The point of my inclusion of her story here is that Gladys was rejected as unsuitable by people who had not effectively designed their hiring requirements.

- They were looking for text book skills not those actually required.
- They hadn't adequately defined the job itself and the environment in which it would have to be accomplished.

Bound by the wisdom of the day that a good Missionary was one strictly trained in an academic manner, they missed the one person most suitable to achieve long-lasting results.

This shouldn't happen to you.

Most of us know what we want
by seeing a lot of what we don't want.

We work backwards to our hiring decisions because, like the Missionary Society, we find it hard to define what is essential for the job we want doing.

Quite apart from deciding these matters about the role itself, we too often forget to add in an evaluation element that screens for those who will thrive in our company, and those who simply won't survive.

Not all of us have the resilience and determination of Gladys. Applying for a new job is a harrowing experience. It feels as if you are being exposed in all your failings when actually you are having the chance to highlight your best points - which for many people is something they find almost impossible to do when nerves overtake them.

Be kind to your applicants.

Respond to everyone who applies. If they are not shortlisted - tell them so. Advertisements that say that the advertising company will only communicate with those who are successful are just reinforcing why people shouldn't want to work there. If they have this attitude to unsuccessful applicants, it is reasonable to expect that these attitudes will be reflected in the company if you join.

You are never too busy to deal with people as individuals, and not as resumés, so don't ever use 'busy' as a reason.

'Too busy' is an excuse. It reveals your true attitude toward valuing people.

The person who applies to your company or whom you interview today may well be in a position of influence for you and your company in the future.

Whether they were successful or not, they should be a willing member of your unpaid marketing team.

They should have good things to say about the experience, because for them that is their only measure of your company.

But that is not the reason to be courteous. It's just the right thing to be. So - some quick reminders on interviewing protocol to achieve that effect:

The Invitation to Interview email or letter.

It should give:

- Directions on finding the interview location together with details about parking - and what the expected charges are, and how they may be paid. Nothing worse than arriving with no coins when that is the only method of payment. Not all parking has a 'phone or card payment option.
- The names of those on the Interview Panel - nervous applicants will probably not remember them when introduced unless they have had a chance to learn names beforehand.
- If you intend to do any tests, say so in your advance letter. Give a general statement about what kind of test: "There will be a test to demonstrate key abilities needed for the job that will take 20 minutes. Please allow for an interview period of 90 minutes when parking".
- Details about any reimbursements for travel to interview and what documentation will be needed, and to whom this should be sent to make a claim, and within what time limit after interview - and how long before the claim will be paid (make it short).

When the interview begins, outline the agenda:

"I'll tell you about the company and where this job sits in the overall plan of things and what we expect to be the outcomes from your work. Then you can tie your background to the job that's been described while we listen and then we'll discuss your background in more detail. Don't mind us writing while you speak. It's important for us to capture things as we go".

This alerts the applicant to listen to the descriptions of company and specifics of the role so he or she can make the best match from their own skills and expertise.

After the interview, follow up as soon as is possible with either a positive or negative response.

Some companies just advise the successful applicant and those who were not successful are expected to work it out from ensuing silence.

This shouldn't be you.

Well done is better than well said.

Benjamin Franklin[41]

---

[41] The 6th President of the United States of America, Benjamin Franklin was a true polymath and inventor who gave us the lightning rod, bifocals, swim fins and a flexible urinary catheter.

Chapter Eight

Making an Impression:

The interview process

Knock Knock.

Who's there?

Opportunity.

Don't be silly – opportunity doesn't knock twice!

Anon

If you are using some sort of competition or online engagement that helps you source the very precise talent needed to do the jobs you need to fill, then the interviewing process has been done for you.

When this is not the case, a guide might help you through something most managers hate to do because it is like orienteering without map or compass – and getting it wrong can lead to everyone feeling lost and wound more than your pride.

Planning the Interview

First of all – a critical point. The people you really want working for you are seeing the interview as a two way street.

You are not the only one interviewing.

Your applicants are interviewing you too.

People work for people, not companies. So be yourself and be passionate about what you do.

The best example I know of an applicant interviewing while being interviewed is when Claire Rhodes interviewed for a senior marketing role on the Woburn Abbey Estate in England.

Woburn Abbey, about one hour north of London is the family home of the Duke of Bedford, but is also open for public visits and events with its magnificent sculpture gallery and gardens, a golf club, Safari Park with world famous breeding program, and a model railway.

During her interview the Duke asked her an interesting question: "Faults?"

She replied: "Yours or Mine?"

Undaunted, he paused before responding: "Good point. I'll go first."Now that is a man you want to work for.

At the time of writing, some 15 years later, Claire is now Commercial Manager for Woburn Golf Club and Woburn Safari Park. She thought so too!

Getting the right person for the job is the single most critical thing you have to do in growing your company – whether it grows fast or slowly.

The right people don't always announce themselves.

Sometimes the right people exclude themselves based on flawed perceptions about their 'rightness' for the job.

Your job is to make your job advertisement one that overcomes this by being the sticky fly paper that the right people want to fly to.

Sometimes the way you search for the right person almost guarantees that you won't find her.

Hiring is full of complexity and the worst part of it is making a good job interview.

You and your team are too busy to review loads of CVs effectively by the methods you're using – so here is a suggested alternative that has been proven to work – and work well.

Remember that this book is a guide – it's not a rule book. Work with your hiring managers and set out your own methods. Scrap these if you come up with something better.

This method is designed to get all the information you need to hire or not to hire.

- You'll be able to justify why you made the decision.
- You'll have been relaxed and professional.
- The candidate will be impressed and relieved.

Less hassle all around!

The worst thing about interviewing is deciding precisely what it is you are looking for, and whether you will know it when you see it.

We need to draw a clear enough picture of what we are looking for to design our interview.

There are several ways to draw a thing, but if you want to do so over and over again with some accuracy, you could use a template. That way you only design once, rather carefully, and then each future design is as accurate on the same model.

Have you ever tried to draw a kangaroo? It's much easier with a template– otherwise you tend to get all sorts of hybrid varieties. The most popular looks like a cross between a beaver and a giraffe – doesn't do a lot for the national image.

An emu? Now that's quite different: a couple of stick legs topped with a fluff of what look like feathers. Add a stick neck and some beady eyes and the thing nearly paces off the page looking for your bag of crisps.

Most of us aren't able to describe what we want as easily as one can draw an emu. Most of us want exotic breeds or exotic mixes. Even these lend themselves to the template approach in designing an interview to select them.

Templates distil the makeup of the breed of person you want. Maybe you need to be realistic and limit the skills you want your applicant to hold and instead hire two people with complementary skills – or match a new set of skills with those of some of the team already resident. That way, together any two make one fine person.

To select your well-fitting person, you'll need two templates, and once you lay one on top of another and add a few suitable questions you have a readymade interview kit.

You are the one who'll be designing the specifications, but this is the method we'll use.

- First, we'll design your company template, and then we design the job template.
- Then you can rummage through some useful questions we provide for you and fit the ones that suit to your template – or add better ones.
- You can then make a fill-in-the-blanks guide for your interviews.
- Using this, you can then interview someone after 10 minutes preparation and know you haven't missed anything crucial.

Templates also help your records of the interview. Records are a legal requirement in many places and they need to reflect a lack of bias of any sort.

That is actually good business sense anyway. Even comments like 'lady in red dress' shouldn't appear.

Limit your notes to answers to the printed questions you have prepared.

Company Description

There are certain environments where each of us performs at our best, and those in which we don't. The job may be the same in your company as in another – or appear to be – but we will succeed in one company and not the other.

If you project this reality to your applicants you are setting the scene for leaving any decision not to hire as one proclaiming a lack of fit rather than an implication that the person isn't up to standard. This can have a less damaging effect on the dignity and self-confidence of a failed applicant.

Companies are not all alike. You've already spent some time describing yours. It will be the basis for the company template company.

This is an example of what the Company Grid can look like. When scoring, if Integrity needs to be High and it was evaluated at Medium, the answer would be NO.

Some jobs require smart personal presentation and impact. If the person is a back room support person...is good presentation that important?

If Commitment can be either at Medium or High put an asterisk in both squares.

Someone may have shown that their commitment was Medium in another company but they may have demonstrated High Commitment in some personal contribution to a community project. It would be fair to put a mark in Medium but expect that in your company, with passion for your outcome, this would move to High. Move your mark in that direction.

The Applicant Description

In describing the job there are often misconstrued requirements assigned. These are used because they have been used on other Job Descriptions and people feel comfortable with them.

These should be challenged for their actual relevance in evaluating ability to do the job in question.

Be clear.

Interview with the possibility that despite your planning of the sequence of questions and answers, sometimes when you are looking for one thing you find another.

Plan how to deal with that, should it happen.

Sample Company Fit Grid

Characteristic	High	Medium	Low
Integrity	●	●	
Sense of humour	●		
Commitment	●	●	
Stand alone ability	●	●	
Flexibility	●		
Presentation skills			●
Technical skills	●	●	

Describe the essential qualities and abilities required to do the job.

_____

_____

_____

_____

_____

_____

_____

Examine the list and distil what is essential.

Now insert these in the blank spaces in the same way, as appropriate. Don't expand the grid! Limit yourself to seven things.

Sample Company Fit Grid

Characteristic	High	Medium	Low

How essential is 'essential'?

Before you blithely play 'Follow the Job Description Leader', decide in all fairness what really is essential and what is desirable.

Few people correctly assign the 'essential' label. Examine the job and its true needs before *you* do.

Ability to meet deadlines

Most jobs have deadlines of some sort.

- Are those for this job critical and cause pressures of time on a regular basis?
- Are there often deadlines of almost equal importance?
- Are they short-notice deadlines or does the person has time to prepare for them?

There are two types of pressures: single and multiple. Some people who can handle a specific deadline for a particular piece of work cannot handle multiple deadlines that fall close together.

Therefore be careful to categorise the type of pressure that a person can handle, and ensure that it reflects the needs of that particular job.

Juggling priorities

People who are good at 'multi-tasking' are often not obviously well organised. Frequently their desks look like the aftermath of a tornado.
Don't confuse orderliness
with the ability to be well-organised.

Sometimes what shows itself as orderly actually reflects a preoccupation with detail that overrides the ability to handle several things at once and know how to adjust so both objectives and their deadlines are met. It shouldn't take a project management qualification to do this. Experience may prove a better evaluation tool.

Following instructions

There are some jobs where the ability to follow instructions precisely is critical.

Some examples are research studies and statistical trials, animal breeding studies, or handling of certain hazardous substances or equipment.

Your jobs might not be that rigorous, but if someone needs to be able to follow instructions, this quality is sometimes hard to pick because there are some people who talk a wonderful story.

Usually, the people who think
they are good at following instructions
are hopeless at it.

Listen to what you have asked at interview and what the candidate answers. Too often the answer is to something other than what you asked. This is could be because of not listening carefully, not understanding, or misinterpreting the question (and not clarifying that they got it right at the outset).

Often, this is a result of hearing the first part of the sentence, second guessing the question and not stopping to actually listen to what followed.

It could be just over confidence. "I know. I know. I have a lot of experience in this field" can be a recipe for disaster.

What your applicant did – or what others did

Speaking about past employment should mean that you quiz people to discover if they were just in the general vicinity of the results being achieved or actually played a part.

If the latter –
- What was their part?
- How did they achieve the results?

- With whom did they need to liaise to do that, and what went wrong, and how was that handled.

It's hard to fake answers to that line of enquiring.

The head of IT in a global Financial Services company was proud to boast of being in a key supervisory role at a well known company at a time of its greatest achievements.

None of those at a peer to peer level dealing with him in his current role thought he demonstrated anything like the skills such a person leading these achievements would have needed to have.

It was generally agreed he may have been in the same building – or as one person suggested, possibly as close as walking down the street outside.

His CV may have looked great to whoever hired him, but judging on his later performance, someone didn't interview carefully.

Similarly, the new head of a Regional Development Agency had absolutely no knowledge of the working environment in which such jobs needed to operate, and showed few ethics in setting up operations.

As an example, unlicensed software was issued with instructions to "Just make a copy." When challenged on the legality of this and the fact that it exposed a multi-funded social enterprise company to copyright infringement, there was hostility in his response and instructions to go ahead.

Pondering why this person was chosen over someone who had obvious relevant experience and credentials of success in the field of economic development, someone answered: "But he was hired because he has such experience in finance. He's an Investment Banker." The response to that statement was: "He's not an Investment Banker or he'd still be an Investment Banker. He worked for an Investment Bank – two different things." Then as an afterthought: "But he did arrange finance for marinas and the Chair of the hiring committee has just got the rights for the local marina, so he's well-qualified for that."

Bottom line:
Hire for the job the person will be paid to achieve
because your hiring decisions
may come back to haunt your own reputation.

Technical skills

What must the person have when they start, and what can be trained?

If you don't actually test the skills needed, ask people actually doing the job now what sorts of questions will quickly show either the necessary skills, or in their absence the type of thinking someone should display in answering the question from the base of other skills.

Language skills

Test them. Don't accept 'Fluent' on a CV as proof of natural speaking competence at a business level.

Ordering a meal in Italian vs. analysing a business problem are two quite different sets of vocabulary.

Interview questions

We've isolated the specifics of what we need.

All we have to do now is to ensure that our interview covers these well enough to establish a measure of whether the applicant holds them at the level we need.

The way to do so is to plan some appropriate questions to include in your discussions with the applicant. These should always be open ended questions.

An open-ended question is one that requires more than a YES/NO answer.

Hypothetical questions are the easiest to answer.

A hypothetical question is one formed in such a way that familiarly accepted facts give a base which anticipates a generalised answer. Such answers are usually of the sort that make generalisations to which everyone would subscribe but that are impossible to precisely define. In those cases it's pretty easy to guess what the expected and acceptable answer would be. Much more revealing is an open-ended question like this:

"Describe a situation where you had to advise a manager that an expected deliverable was going to be delayed, and tell us what happened."

Some people talk a good prepared story but it's very hard to keep up the window-dressing in answering sequential questions of:

- Describe...
- How did it work when...?
- Why?
- How did you know it was effective?
- In retrospect, why you think this was the best thing to do?
- Why not?
- What were other alternatives?
- What sort of impact did that have?

If there is something that just puzzles you, and you are unsure how authentic a previous answer has been, try the 'Door Handle Close'. It's a great sales tool that applies well at interview when clarification is sought.

The way it works is this: The interview appears to have finished and the candidate is getting ready to leave. When the candidate reaches for the door handle, you delay departure with "Oh, by the way – just one more question."

The applicant has mentally left the interview and is more relaxed. The answer given spontaneously in response to a question posed then is usually more honest because of that.

Just because you've prepared a series of questions, if the applicant has covered those answers in answering another question, that's good enough.

Their earlier points may need further clarification, but you need to adapt your plan.

Motto: Be flexible.

One question I always ask towards the end of the interview is: "Why you? Why do you think you are the best candidate for the role?"

This gives the person a chance to fit themselves to your company and the role itself from their perspective, not yours. It also shows how much homework they have done on your company – or even on you. It's something I ask at the end. That way the answer also can illustrate how well the applicant listened to the overview of the company and the role.

Justin Nowak, VP, Community & Events, Canadian Cloud Council uses an unusual question to see if someone will make up any old answer, use logic and reasoning, or be honest and say they don't know but will find out and get back with the answer.

The question is 'Why are manhole covers round?'

Microsoft used the same question to evaluate logic and creativity in the answers. Because Microsoft used it, others followed suit. This has devalued its currency because some people rehearse the possible answers 'just in case'. Some of these possible answers are now even on Wikipedia.

However, this is a good illustrative example and perhaps you and your team can devise something of the same type that is uniquely yours.

Just as these answers listed below show the range of possibility, you should gather a list of some plausible answers to the similar question your team devises. Keep adding to it as inventive candidates show ingenuity beyond that of your team, and you.

If you use the manhole cover question be aware that it may have been prepared for. Rapidity of answering is a giveaway. But is it bad to prepare for any eventuality?

That is up to you to answer because it depends why you are asking the question. If it's to test the ability to think creatively, limit the question to those you need to do so.

There may be some tasks where creativity is not needed, in fact quite the opposite: editing documentation is one of them.

If you are testing for logic, give the person time to think. This is what in parliamentarian terms is called a 'Question without notice.' Put another way – some people think ponderously but their thinking is soundly analytical.

Apart from the straightforward answers about why manhole covers are round, possible answers could be:

- Although there is a lip and therefore any shape could work, a round cover can't accidentally fall down the hole because it can't be placed on an angle.
- A triangle or curve of constant width would work, but a round cover is easier to manufacture.
- Round tubes are the safest because they are strongest and efficient against compression in the earth so a round tube would naturally have a round cover.
- The load-bearing surfaces of manholes are carefully machined to be flat enough not to be dislodged by traffic.
- Round castings are easier to machine on a lathe than angled ones.
- It is easy to move by rolling.
- They don't need to be rotated to fit.
- Smaller surface of round vs square means less material, lower cost.
- They can be easily locked by a quarter turn so they can only be opened with a particular tool. If locked they can be lighter because they can't be dislodged by the suction of passing traffic.

Someone might even have done research and know that some manhole covers in Nashua New Hampshire are triangular and point in the direction of flow. Did anyone suggest there may be other shapes in use but not recorded or widely known?

That would be the person who tries to be aware that there may be a black swan, even though to date all swans have only been white. To put that in another way – will make contingencies for the unexpected.

Your logic question should have similar qualities in seeking creative answers. Someone should keep a log of the creative answers that emerge. Give each such question a lifespan and when that is reached find another. Then publish the list of creative answers to the one that is being retired.

Have your teams vote on the best, funniest, most logical, etc. – and award prizes to the people who came up with them. If the one they vote the best isn't from someone you hired, is it worth reconsidering that decision?

Here are some examples of open-ended questions on certain skills or aptitudes that may help you formulate your own.

They are only meant to be a guide and are grouped under subject headings for easy reference.

Sample interview questions
Ambition

- What are your goals for self development?
- What have you achieved towards these in the last year?
- What were your career goals within X organisation?
- When did you formulate them?
- What progress did you make, and how?
- Have you defined a future path?
- If so, what have you accomplished towards it in the last 12-18 months?
- What do you still need to do to accomplish this?
- What are your strengths?
- How are you capitalising on them?
- How can these work to benefit both you and our company?
- Have you taken any skills development courses recently?
- If YES, when? Where? How? Who suggested it? Who paid for it?
- If you had more spare time, what would you do with it?
- How would you describe your ambitions?
- What would you like to be known to have achieved during your work life?
- As a person?

Analytical ability

- What kind of reports do you prepare in your job?
- What sorts of information do they contain, and who reads them?
- How do you prepare them?
- Describe the role you have in decision-making in your organisation.
- What sort of analytics do you prepare? Are they effective? How do you know?
- Describe a situation where you have unexpectedly had to make a decision that would normally have been made by your supervisor/manager.

- How did that situation arise?
- Why did you make the decision you did?
- In hindsight was it the right decision? Why or why not?
- What factors did you have to take into consideration?
- What is the biggest mistake you have ever made in analysing data?
- In hindsight is there anything you could have done differently given the information you had at the time?
- With information that later became available how would the decision you made have been different?
- What is the most effective analysis of information you have ever made, and why was it important?
- Describe a situation where you have had to make a rapid decision about priorities, knowing that there were risks attached to getting it wrong.
- Include what those risks were and the penalties associated with them.

Communications ability
Verbal communications

The best assessment of these skills is how the candidate responds at interview.

Select from the candidate's interests if already listed on the CV to elicit what these interests are: then form some questions around them.

The answers also give you some indication of passion about a subject – that may indicate the opportunity to generate similar passion about your company objective.

If you then hire this candidate, when you meet in the first week of employment (if possible) ask how these interests can benefit from your company. If the person is taken aback and can't think of anything, get the results of later thought sent to you by email. It does give you a bit of extra work, but there is no better way to show a new member of your team that you listened and are interested in what they care about.

It can also harness a whole new unpaid marketing team for the company.

If there is no way to accommodate the initial suggestion, get someone in your team with the authority to do so to take up the conversation to find something else.

Then make sure it happens.

- What are the benefits of being a member of the Lions Club?

Possible link: Lions Clubs and other organisations benefit the community through their work.

There may be a fund raiser held internally by a team putting together a small lunchtime event for which people pay to participate.

- In your bird/train/plane spotting activities what was the best or the most unexpected find?

Possible link: Perhaps one of your clients is Airbus, or Amtrak or the Simplon Express, or a major airline. Introduce the person to a client representative with a view to arranging a tour for all who wish to join from your team. You might even tie in a short presentation on their processes for handling decision making – or problem resolution.

- What are the duties of a Cycle/Little League/Football club/Chicken Breeding Association Chairman/Treasurer?

Possible link: With this experience perhaps the person can illustrate new techniques or perspectives from those you use in your company.

Can this offer a learning opportunity about how to run meetings, engage people to get something done, manage budgets, etc.? If so, then team the person with someone who can help them deliver something meaningful – done in the style of whatever club they talk about. You get the idea!

Instructional communication

If instructional communication is absolutely critical, it should be tested. There are several ways to do so and they each involve a written task that has to be described in such a way that all who hear the instructions act accordingly to achieve the end result desired. One I have used is to give the person a blank piece of paper on which all the folds to make a paper aeroplane are clearly marked on one side.

The task is to describe the folds and the sequences so the listeners all have a flying model. It may sound easy but it does require some thought before starting to speak so that the ensuing instructions are simple, unambiguous, and in the right sequence.

This can be a light-hearted exercise – but you will need time to do it. Keep the atmosphere informal and that will reduce the pressure. The way the candidate responds to the way the audience gets it right or wrong is also part of your evaluation of how they fit with your company.

General communication questions

These are example questions and all are not applicable to all roles. They do show that a sequence of questions drills down to the bedrock of reality and shatters a superficial layer of good-sounding but not factual claims.

- Describe a situation where something quite technical or complex has been explained by you or someone else to a non-technical person who has had difficulty understanding. How did it end up?
- Describe any public speaking engagement you've done that you really enjoyed.
- What was the purpose of the talk?
- What made you think you achieved that, or didn't?
- Describe the most challenging and confrontational exchange you ever had with someone at work or with a client. What caused their anger?
- Was it justified?
- How did you calm things down and what was the outcome?

Written communication

The CV you are working from may have been prepared by someone else other than the candidate. The best test is to pose a situation to which someone needs to respond in writing and evaluate the response. Here are some sample questions to supplement the written test.

- Would you rather give a written or a verbal report? Why?
- What is the most challenging business letter you have had to write and how did you manage it?

Creativity and innovation

This is your chance to get input into what you can do to create the best environment where innovation and creativity flourish. It may be worth saying that before you ask the questions designed to evaluate them.

- What is different about your job now, from when you first started?
- How did those changes come about?
- What is the most innovative thing you have created or done in any field – at work or socially in your own time?
- How much opportunity for innovation is there in your current job?
- Why?
- What sort of environment helps you create your most creative results?
- Is that something you can easily set up yourself or what could we do to make that possible?
- What do you do to find blocks of quiet time you need to block out distractions? Work from home? Library? Some other place or environment?

- What improvements would you make to improve your immediate work area or methods? What improvements would you expect from those changes?

Decisiveness and judgement

What you are seeking here are answers that show whether the candidate saw all the available options and why the particular course of action was taken.

- Give examples of the sorts of decisions you make spontaneously and those that require some further consideration.
- Give an example of a good decision you made in... job.
- What were the alternatives?
- Why was it a good decision?
- How are the boundaries to your authority to make decisions in your current job defined?
- In what circumstances can that vary?
- Has that ever happened, and if so what took place and what was the outcome?

Delegation methods and organisational abilities

The level of control the candidate holds versus the level of autonomy he gives to others should be measured against the role for which you are hiring.

Someone controlling a scientific experiment needs to retain a different level of control from someone organising a product launch or managing HR.

- Who is acting for you while you are out of the office?
- Why did you select that person?
- What guidelines does that person have to help in decision making?
- Who did you advise that this person would be able to take responsibility in your absence?
- What keeps you from delegating more?
- How do you decide what is worth delegating and what is better for you to do yourself?
- We all have different ways of working, and each has its merits. Do you work best on seeing one thing at a time to a well organised clear end result, or on handling several things at once? Both have positives to them and we can use both skills.
- What could we do to help you to achieve that?
- Describe an example that is typical of how you work at your best.

- How do you keep track of things that need to be handled at a later date?

Development of subordinates

The last question is an interesting one and you can devise your own version. People trying to impress you will often give the name of someone who you will recognise, to show their importance.

Someone who really takes pride in seeing another person flourish will give a true account of mentoring or their ability to inspire a person it is unlikely that you would ever know or have heard of.

That is just one aspect of what an answer to these questions may reveal, but it is an interesting one.

- How do you evaluate the development needs of the people who work for you?
- If you leave who will replace you?
- Will that be the result of your influence? Explain.
- What are the two most common training needs of your team?
- How will they be accomplished?
- What training would you like to take to further develop your leadership skills?
- How could we help you do that?
- Other than family members, tell us about the person on whom you have made the greatest impact in your work or life over the years and why you think you did have an impact.

Empathy

Empathy is that thing that:

- tells you that people like personal space
- helps you recognise that people who say little often have much to contribute but are reluctant to do so in some environments
- causes you to help someone struggling with a heavy package by opening the door for them – unasked, and
- causes you to not park in the disabled parking spot at the all night supermarket thinking the users for whom it is designated couldn't possibly need it after dark.

Empathy is why people don't bully others and why they support other people's triumphs and applaud their achievements.

How important empathy is to your company is up to you to decide. Be thoughtful in your response.

If you have been told you are low on empathy yourself – maybe you need to surround yourself with people who have more of it than you do.

That will be challenging, but will most probably improve life for you, your family and those you care about personally, as well as making a happier work environment.

Here are some useful ideas for questions about empathy:

- Describe an unpopular decision you have had to make.
- What responses did you get?
- Why did people respond like that?
- What are you and your colleagues most proud of?
- Describe a situation where you have been frustrated by the responses of a supervisor. What happened?

Flexibility, resilience, tenacity and stress tolerance

Evaluate how a person has managed to cope with diverse types of circumstances. It is one thing to be able to excel or keep improving in one specialised skill, and that has its own value.

However, if a person has worked in different fields and has a track record of success in more than one, this is a different measure with its own value for the reliance and adaptability it reflects.

- Describe a situation when you had to work around obstacles that seemed likely to prevent the successful completion of a project.
- When you made the change from (doing a different job from that which the candidate now holds) how did you approach that?
- Describe the project that took the longest time to complete.
- Was that within its planned timeframe or had it extended? How did you handle that?
- What gives you the most stress in your current job? How do you handle it?
- What was the biggest obstacle you had to overcome to get where you are today?
- How did you overcome it?
- Most jobs end up being something rather different than what was described at interview. What has changed in your current job since you started?
- How do you feel about those changes?
- Have you been involved in them?
- What was the worst career setback that you ever had?
- Why is it the worst?
- Most things have some benefit: what was the good thing that came out of it?
- What happened afterwards?
- How has that influenced your career direction?

Taking notes

A good piece of advice I have applied ever since receiving it when working in Executive Search for Burnett Personnel in Houston, Texas, I share with you for consideration: Never write on someone's CV.

Many HR specialists make this clear to all interviewers for the reason that writing on the CV is something spontaneous and recording responses or impressions impulsively can lead to thoughtless memory prompts or observations that may indicate bias.

It is useful to bear in mind that, should you be challenged to do so, interview records are your proof that you made an equitable decision based on the facts. This makes good sense. However there is another reason for not writing on a person's CV.

In many cultures any image of you is an element of you – so a photograph, business card, and your Curriculum Vitae are all manifestations of you and when casually handled or written upon, this indicates disrespect of the person. Subliminally this may also be how each of us feels as well.

Respect your candidate.
That is what I was taught.
Pass it on.

Those of you doing business internationally should always check the protocols of this nuance. For example, casually handling a Japanese Executive's Business Card is seen as most disrespectful. It should be taken in both hands, read attentively, placed carefully on the desk or in your folder with a slight bow and your card handed over with the same dignity.

Write your notes in spaces under your prepared questions and omit descriptive hints to yourself as to who was who – even things that seem quite innocent as a memory jogger.

Whether for legal reasons or out of respect – both reasons have value.

For both reasons - don't.

Looking for the right person

Try not to limit your expectations of what sort of package a person comes in.

Sometimes some that seem unprepossessing at first turn out to be the unexpected diamonds you wish you had found when you see them glittering in someone else's company.

Be flexible.

Prepare your interviews so they aren't exhausting for you or the candidate. Make it an experience they remember positively. It will take the stress out of it for you as well.

Let the tone of the interview reflect the tone of the company – with the caveat that if your development team plays bongos and flicks paper at each other while they plan, don't try to emulate that!

I'm not weird.

I'm a limited edition

Anon

Chapter Nine

Migration and integration.

Settling new employees
...welcome to my house.

Come freely.

Go safely;
and leave something of the happiness you bring.

Bram Stoker[42]

Remember your first day at senior school?

Remember the awkwardness of not knowing the system, not knowing too many people, not understanding how to get places within the grounds – all those things that made you feel so vulnerable?

Well this is how your new starters feel!

If you want them to be quickly productive, you need to make them feel at home, know where to find things, and know where the boundary fences lie.

To do that requires a bit of planning – once.
Then you have a system and backup documents that will save you and your existing team endless queries and interruptions.
Get your team together and ask them what was hardest for them when each of them started and from that list you have the start of what is important for new starters in your organisation.
Consider some of these options to help settle in the new immigrants to your tribe:

---

[42] Bram Stoker, author of Dracula, was an Irish writer whose day job was as manager of the Lyceum, one of the most important of London's theatres at the time. He was also personal secretary to the owner, Henry Irving, and in his company travelled the world, visiting the White House and knowing both Presidents McKinley and Roosevelt.

Start before the new person arrives.

Send a welcome letter – a personal one from you at the top. In it give:

- Dress code
- Expected arrival time, how to gain an access pass if required, and who to ask for upon arrival.
- Designate which office entrance to use if there are several entrances, or separate buildings.
- Information about Public Transport access to the office.
- Directions for driving to the office and parking.
- If the parking area requires a Parking Permit, include it in the letter. If the parking area is external, advise how the person can pay for parking (have coins of a certain denomination ready – pay by 'phone or card, etc) and whether there is a reimbursement plan for the fees paid or not.
- If there is to be a company car to be issued, be sure to advise when that will be available and how that process will work, so the new applicant can arrange the appropriate transport in the meantime.
- A description of lunch options, or if you have arranged the first day(s) to have lunch hosted – say so.
- Outline the proposed Agenda for Day One.

On the first day:

Have the new person's business cards on the desk. Nothing says 'Welcome' better

- Have the person's greeter properly briefed on the new arrival and his or her new role.
- The greeter should give a tour of all the facilities – and this should include meeting senior members of staff. The tour should include details about how things work. Do you have access codes for photocopiers? Have you an honour system for the tea and coffee, or how does that all work?
- Have the person's supervisor list out the 30, 60, 90 day expectations of the role. This helps people feel they have a pathway they can follow rather than valiantly pursuing what they think to be the right focus of activities only to find they have not met other expectations.
- Have some simple tasks ready to be completed and a support person nearby to help with any questions. There are many Log In

requirements and registration on this system and that, and other things necessary for a new hire to establish even before any work can be started. Make sure the new person isn't left to work all these out alone.

- A simple check list of what a new starter needs to complete in order to be functional, together with a guide as to how to accomplish them is a good starting point. It will also save you and your team lots of time in repetitive explanations as more newcomers arrive.
- Arrange a lunch with a new staff member for three days within the first week. Make sure the lunch hosts are at peer level, below, and above. Decide if you pay or they each pay for their own and make sure both parties understand the rules whatever they are.

Tailor what you do to your company.
Don't do it because you read it here or anywhere else.
This is your company.
Make it colourfully so – but keep it
the sort of thing that sits naturally in your company.

Instead of having each new staff member write out a short summary of interests, have them make a pictorial collage of interests, favourite places, sports, pets, etc. This could be brought with them on arrival.

Make a portfolio of collages from all your existing team and include these in your welcome pack. This makes an opportunity to establish a non-work point of common interest between the team you have and the new arrival.

Your greeter should be responsible for reviewing the new arrival's collage and making appropriate introductions to anyone having a like interest.

Find out any languages spoken other than English and match to other team members with the same language skills.

A salutary example here. No point in having these skills listed if you don't think creatively about using them!

A fast growing software company hosting a visit by potential banking clients from Finland had a senior programmer who understood the system well and for whom Finnish is her native language. She was never invited to be the greeter, special liaison – nothing. She sat in a room twenty metres from the visiting group and never met them.

Could the loss of that sale have been avoided by a warmer and more thoughtful presence from someone who could speak the language of the client, and understand the nuances of response in a way the English team never could?

They will never know. They didn't close the contract with the biggest and most influential bank in the Baltic area. One can only feel that there was a missed opportunity there. When asked before the meeting about including her because of these language skills, the VP Sales had scoffed at her inclusion being relevant. She was a senior programmer with a great deal of experience about the system being promoted, so not so irrelevant, but in his eyes only salespeople should be present.

But this was the same VP who refused to believe his own HR when they advised the due process for closing an office in France.

When so advised he stated "I've never done it that way, and not about to start now." That cost over one million Euros in legal penalties.

So two lessons here:

- Be creative about using the extra skills your team members have, and
- Follow the advice you are given if it is properly researched and sets out your legal obligations.

Your opinion of the legalities under which you must operate is irrelevant. Ignore them at your peril – and at your cost.

So now you have pondered some of these ideas, describe how this will work for you and how your staff will settle in quickly and become productive.

You may have a short introduction document that explains the company, its structure, benefits and how it works – and most importantly, how to work in it. If not, have someone on the staff develop one. Once you have drawn it up, buy everyone an office lunch to be eaten in-house while you each look at it and throw in comments and criticisms. Incorporate the important missing elements and you will have a pretty decent induction that reflects the character of your company.

Beware of the current management hype about a practice that has been successful somewhere. Somewhere isn't here. Here is where you have built something that reflects your aspirations and culture – and you've hired people who fit with it.

Tinker by adding something that worked somewhere else at your peril.

Why it worked there may have more to do with the fit it has within the context of that company: its history, style and the attitudes and expectations of the people within it.

That is why this theme is repeated throughout the book:

You got this far with your team making up the answers.
Why can't they still do that?

They may benefit from some guidance but the best answers come from within. It might be that you just need help identifying key issues and refining focus so these answers evolve.

Settling In

There are many ways of making people feel comfortable – or making them feel comfortable to say they have self-selected as not being a fit to the company they just joined. Your style should be reflected in whatever option you choose: but choose one!

People have to feel that they belong. Only when they do will they have the courage to metaphorically thump the desk of the most senior manager and point out the error of her ways.

Thump the desk?

I did say: "Metaphorically".

Why?

The way I used to explain it was that in a rapidly growing company, management has its hands full. They need to manage the moment and the future, and the future is already upon them with untold new demands every day. So management maintains a total focus on the objectives to which they are headed in order not to be drawn irrevocably away from the goal.

I used to relate it to walking across a cliff top, taking the shortest route – though often a precarious one, towards a specific point on the horizon. As the Management Team head across the ridge they occasionally dislodge a stone or two due to the pace at which they are travelling. They never stop to look back at where they have been. Their focus is ahead. Therefore, they never notice that those few stones start an avalanche on the poor souls below. But the avalanche is reality to the people below, for while they are busy coping with the avalanche everything else goes on hold.

Unless every staff member, even the most junior person, or the newest, feels comfortable enough to tell management they are causing avalanches they will keep doing so.

How do you get them that comfortable, quickly?

We used to hold a Murder Mystery Night every few months, or whenever we had between ten and twenty new employees who had started in the last short while. The new starters attended as did the entire

HR team and it was mandatory for all Managers and Directors to attend, including the MD.

Each Manager or Director was paired up with a new staff member who didn't work for them – the most senior manager with the most junior employee. Any leftover member of the Management Team formed teams of three with the new employees and other managers. Other than those mentioned, established staff could not attend. This was a bonding night between new employees and management.

The Murder Mystery itself was designed by the existing staff. They had to decide which staff member to kill and devise their preferred method. But before they could actually use that person as the murder victim, they had to gain his or her permission to be killed, and also get agreement on the method of death. It seems only fair after all.

But what we were doing here was more than introducing the new staff to the senior management in a fun environment.

This concept made it acceptable to approach someone who was becoming unpopular and explain why the rest of the staff wanted to murder them. By asking their permission, they engaged the person in the solution and in an interchange of some energy regarding the nature of the position they were in.

Often, the critics found that the potential victim had frustrations with them also.

It became an acceptable forum to sort out what may have otherwise escalated to a higher level of frustration.

For the event, a buffet dinner and drinks were provided and the teams were set the clues and had to interview each other to come to some sort of conclusion. There were prizes for the funniest, the most irreverent, the cleverest, the most bizarre, the most unlikely – and the correct solution.

Remember that all the new starters had actually been working in their jobs for a few weeks. They actually vaguely knew the person who was being killed. For this reason we made a point of explaining that the person had been involved with the staff planning team who designed this evening's mystery. We made it clear that they had together evolved decisions about his or her impending demise.

Here, we stressed the realities of fast growth and explained that from time to time we were each candidates for the corpse-in-question, because we were each trying our best to get maximum result in compressed time – and sometimes causing major aggravations along the way.

This also contributed to setting the tone of the company. It said "We know that we do things badly sometimes and that you want to shoot us – and that is understandable. But we also are prepared to stand up and explain ourselves and for others to understand the reasons why we act as we do so that together sort out some workable way forward."

None-the-less, people sometimes wrote very personal things, hurtful things, vindictive things, about the murder victim. These were never readout with the winning entries: and we tried to make as many winners as we could.

We used to announce that if there were any inappropriate solutions submitted – things that could be seen as attacks on the person or personality, or things that were crude, they would be eliminated from the judging. We actually destroyed the very few we received.

This set the tone of what was, and was not, acceptable in our company.

Prizes were silly little items appropriate to the company or the individuals, but suitable to sit on a desk in the future as a reminder of the event.

These prizes were of the enduring kind – specifically designed to be relatively inexpensive but of good quality – reflecting the general ethos of value that the event was endorsing.

Again, that is one method.
Your team can develop its own.

Which bring us to Rule Number 3.

Rule Number 3

Protect the dignity of every individual.

We are talking about people who are working all the hours God sends to get the results you want and need.

They are doing their best.
They are tired.

What some people think of as teasing can really rankle with people when they have given genuine effort above and beyond normal expectations, yet made a stupid mistake - or said something inane - or whatever.

This is **not** the time to take pot shots at each other.

There is a fine line between acceptable joking and getting personal. Hard to define, but you feel it as if someone said "Ouch!"

We also expected everyone to have a sense of occasion.

What is appropriate with the lads at the pub is not necessarily appropriate, in language or content, at a company event - no matter how casual the company may seem.

Our managers used to say that after a Murder Mystery Night the confidence and comfort levels of our new employees was noticeably improved. They felt 'at home'.

How can you integrate your staff so they quickly feel they belong and they 'own' the company?

An expert is a person who has made every possible mistake in a small field of study.

Anon

Chapter Ten

A fine brew: distilling the essential

Start where you are.

Use what you have.

Do what you can.

Arthur Ashe[43]

You bought this book so you could start where you are.

We've started to use what you have by helping isolate what is, and what should be in the future if your company is going to have the right sort of organisational structure to suit its particular personality and needs.

We've prompted you to think about its style, its brand, the way things are done around here and about how your senior team is behaving now and possibly needs to change to adapt to the growth needs of the company.

Now we come to the bit about actually doing something based on all this information!

List what needs to be done in the next 3 months:

_____

_____

_____

_____

_____

[43] Ashe was the first black tennis player on the US Davis Cup Team and the only black man to ever win the singles of Wimbledon, The Australian Open, and the US Open. He contracted HIV from contaminated blood during bypass surgery and before his death went on to use his fame to help others suffering with HIV AIDS.

_____

_____

_____

_____

_____

_____

_____

_____

_____

_____

_____

_____

_____

Now place an * against the two most important thing

Now the next step.

Identify the immediate needs you have to accomplish in the next six months:

_____

_____

_____

_____

_____

_____

_____

_____

_____

_____

_____

_____

_____

_____

_____

_____

_____

_____

Now place an * against the two most important things.

As that timeless person 'Anonymous' once wrote:

Chase two rabbits and both will escape.

Those asterisks have forced you to choose a focus. Focus will distil what is critical. There have been many excellent books written about the importance of focus, and how to be better at it. These are some common points:

- If you have a focus on the long term and resist the urge to be reactive, you will reduce the amount of time needed to fix things because your work will be on the things that prevent most of them happening in the first place.
- Remove the pings and vibrations that your technology is sending to you and concentrate solely on the task at hand.
- Set a time to answer emails each day and stick to it. If something is truly urgent, the person concerned will call, not email.
- Similarly – if you really need an answer – pick up the phone. If you make agreement on a course of action by doing so – but whatever the outcome – if it was important enough to have the discussion in the first place, afterwards send an email confirming

exactly what you believe took place and what conclusions were arrived at and ask for this to be confirmed or edited. The likelihood of two people coming to different conclusions about what was agreed is slim without this double-check.

- When seeking key information, ask yourself if Google is the right first point of reference, or if talking to a person with useful experience might be better.
- Information overload has a negative effect on focus – it breeds too many options.
- Before you start to respond to anything urgent, take a few moments to clarify the elements of the situation – and keep your response limited to those points
- Before seeking answers think through the underlying questions – the root cause of why you need the answer(s). We live in a world where symptoms masquerade very effectively as causes. As was pointed out by the neuroscientist David Marr[44]:

You don't learn how birds fly by studying feathers.
You need to study aerodynamics

- When faced with decisions, there is a roughly even chance that a random decision will be as good as that carefully considered. In Malcolm Gladwell's book 'Blink: The Power of Thinking without Thinking,'[45] he gives examples that demonstrate that if you are immersed in your field of expertise, your instant decision is probably right.
- There are various variations on General George Patton's belief that a good plan executed violently now, is better than a perfect plan executed next week.
- Another famous US General and later President, Dwight D. Eisenhower, left us with a great tool for focus.

---

[44] British neuroscientist David Marr influenced the early development of computational neuroscience by combining results from psychology, artificial intelligence, and neurophysiology to develop new models of visual processing. He stressed the importance of context. Sadly, he died of leukaemia at the age of 35.
www.kybele.psych.cornell.edu/~edelman/marr/marr.html

[45] Blink: The Power of Thinking Without Thinking ISBN 10: 0316010669; ISBN 13: 9780316010665

*It is important to be able to distinguish between
what is important, and what is urgent.*

*What is important is seldom urgent,
and what is urgent is seldom important.*

Remind yourself of that when you scamper off to fix something that only you can fix in your fast growing company.

In a medium sized and fast growing UK company, a Chief Information Officer (CIO) of a software house has a habit of going straight to the customer when there is an issue he perceives to be important. If the customer calls in a tizzwoz, the CIO drops everything and heads off to the customer site. He calls this being 'Customer Focused'.

Such reactive behaviour sends some interesting messages. It tells the customer that the CIO has no oversight of his own system, no trust in his implemented system, and/or no trust in the team who are implementing the solution. If he did, he would respond in a calm and measured manner instead of hopping in the car with no detailed information or context and a God-complex that assures him that only he can fix the problem.

While he is being his version of Customer Focused, this CIO's team is held back from proceeding with work to actually address the problem, or to continue with other work, because this same God-complex CIO doesn't allow them to have any autonomy in decision making. They must get everything signed off by him.

It sounds far-fetched but it is an all too common scenario. You don't act like that do you? If you do it's no wonder you have shrapnel pock marks on your walls.

Remember Lee Iacocca: ' I hire good people and then get out of their way'?

If you have any of the tendencies described here as being less than desirable for a leader of a growing company, you won't be the first.

If you do something about what you learn about yourself –that also won't be a first – but you will be in an elite group of people prepared to be honest with themselves about how they act in reality vs. how they always thought they acted.

It is easy to think you are a warm empathetic person but your teams may find that description one they wouldn't apply.

Check out the mirror and accept that we all make real lash-ups while we are learning to be better. It's what you do about making the future better that counts – not focusing on the clangers of the past.

Accept that the mistakes of today are part of being human and fallible like the rest of us mere mortals.

Dare to change.
Your company will benefit.
Your family and friends will benefit,
and you will definitely benefit.

Important or Urgent?

Thinking something is important but when examined it proves to be urgent is an easy way to lose focus. You've probably seen this decision matrix[46] shown here, courtesy of Wikimedia Commons.

		Urgent	Non-Urgent	
Do it Now	Important	Crying Baby Kitchen Fire Some Calls	Exercise Vocational Planning	Schedule, Do ASAP
Delegate or Eliminate	Not Important	Interruptions Distractions Other Calls	Trivia Busy Work Time - Wasters	Minimise, Eliminate

Keeping focus on what is core to your business helps guide all your decisions and will save you time and effort.

The distinction about which of the 'some calls' fall into Important and Urgent, and which fall into Not Important but Urgent is where the CIO mentioned above lost out.

For many people in management, the adrenalin rush of the Urgent is what stokes their decision making: it makes them feel important and powerful.

This is a massive self-deception.

Ask yourself the honest question of whether sometimes this is you. If it is, continue at your peril.

You are removing the accountability you have assigned to your team members – and if you have ever had someone ask you to do

[46] By Rorybowman [Public domain], from Wikimedia Commons

something and then had them come and take away your ability to do so by doing it themselves, you know the feeling.

It's a fast way to lose high performing people.

The measure of success is not
whether you have a tough problem to deal with,
but whether it is the same problem you had last year.

John Foster Dulles[47]

Focus activities on Box 2, but regarding 'Planning' bear in mind the piece of advice from General Patton in Point 7, (above) – the bit about a good plan now versus a perfect plan next week.

Quadrant One
DISARM: Activity here responds to necessity

DO: These are the things where some immediate action removes stress: Child being injured; last minute rehearsals of key presentations, or other last minute refinements of imminent activities; advice of contractual failure; fire in the building.

These are things that need your decision before they can go ahead or to which an adequate response has a decision from you as its key or requires a response from someone legally accountable for the company.

This may even be a customer complaint or request direct to you – and not just something others are dealing with and about which you are just being kept informed. Even this may prove to need investigation to discover if your intervention is required to defuse the situation.

Fire in the building only needs your involvement AFTER the fire drill, not during - unless you are one of the Fire Wardens.

Remember you are steering, not rowing.

---

[47] JF Dulles was for six years a controversial US Secretary of State who though often criticised (notably by the French, the Brits and India), when he departed was universally described as 'indispensible' by those who had criticised as well as his advocates.

Quadrant Two

DECIDE: This activity is about Quality & Leadership

SCHEDULE: To do

These are the things that contribute to successfully achieving your goals.

Schedule when to do it as soon as you can without conflicting with activities in quadrant one. If time is well spent here it should minimise the number of things in Quadrant one.

These are the long term activities of steering your ship, building roadmaps and relationships – and of looking after your own health and recreation.

Quadrant Three

DELEGATE: This is the Quadrant of Deception

AVOID: Or do later

These are the small interruptions that most of us are happy to spend time on because they're often quite entertaining, and the interruptions make us feel needed and important.

This is where the Last In – First Out Trap appears. There is merit in dealing with something immediately upon reading, because this means it's done.

However, it may take so long to work down that list it may be better to scan incoming mail – email and hard copy – and break into one of three categories:
- Do it now
- Do it later, or
- Get it done.

Quadrant Four

DELETE: The Quadrant of Waste

ELIMINATE, MINIMISE, or *RE-EVALUATE*: Pick two!

This is where Facebook, Snapchat, Pinterest, WhatsApp, Twitter and other social media sit.

Try to minimise involvement such distractions during work hours. This requires discipline to limit time that can be better spent on things that impact your life.

Of course this assumes that you have a home life that is more rewarding than that online. If it's not, maybe you need to spend more time in the Home Quadrant of Not Urgent but Important and rebuild relationships with children and spouse or partner.

Your dog will love you no matter what,
but your development of your fast growth company
may well be testing your other relationships.

If activity on Social Media constitutes relaxation time: great. Schedule it outside your working day. A vital point to make, however:

Sometimes time spent not doing anything visibly related
to the solution of a problem is the best investment.

Cross over thinking

According to an article by Tom McKeag in The Biomicry Column of Green Biz[48], in 1990 engineering design benefited from a lecture by an engineer who described how bird flight relates to design.

A Bullet Train Senior Engineer, Eiji Nakatsu, was then wrestling with the problem the Shinkansen Bullet Train was causing with noise.

As his trains emerged from tunnels, their connection with the overhead electrical wires was causing sonic booms that could be heard 400 meters (about 437 yards -or a bit over a quarter of a mile) away. Another noise problem was caused by the fast movement through the air that amplified the train's normal noise as it travelled.

Following the lecture, Nakatsu applied his thinking to birds. He remembered the noise-softening wing feathers of an owl that enable it to arrive upon its prey so unexpectedly.

By emulating owl feather design his new train designs reduced the train's progress noise so that was able to comply with the stringent noise standards of the Japanese government.

The sonic booms proved more complex. They had a dual cause – both the forcing of air from the tunnel ahead of the train as well as the way it connected to the overhead wire.

The problem therefore had relevance to both the shape of the tunnel and the speed of the train. A junior engineer talked with him about

---

[48] How one engineer's bird watching made Japan's bullet train better: Tom McKeag 19 Oct,2012 www.greenbiz.com/blog/2012/10/19/how-one-engineers-birdwatching-madejapans-bullet-train-better

the problem, and observed that it seemed as if the train shrank as it travelled through the tunnel. They concluded that this must be due to the rapidity of the change from open air to closed tunnel.

This proved a vital prompt to Nakutsu's memory. An avid birdwatcher, he recalled dive of a kingfisher that travels at great speed from air into water with barely a splash. Both air and water are classified as fluids in that they both flow, but water is eight hundred times denser.

Nakutsu realised that it must be the shape of the kingfisher's bill that enabled this elegant ease of almost frictionless penetration.

Not only did the new design that emulated the kingfisher bill reduce the sonic boom, but the new trains using it were able to travel faster because of less air resistance, travelling for the first time at speeds of up to 300mph.

Even the train's recessed headlights reflect the placement and design of the kingfisher's nostrils.

If you have ever travelled on such a fast train it is a surreal experience. I stood before the small digital speed display on the Deutsche Bahn train as it whisked me from Frankfurt to Paris and was thrilled to see it reach 300mph.At that moment it felt more stable than many other commuter trains.

It was even more exciting than when in the early 1980s I rode in one of the first Shinkansen Bullet Trains in the very front seat from Tokyo to Furukawa Station en route to Naruko Onsen, the home of Kokeshi dolls.

Kokeshi dolls are marvels of fine design in wood and Naruko Onsen is their source. It's a trip worth making. The modernity of the bullet train ride is in direct contrast to the graciousness of the ancient mountain town. But I digress.

Without Nakutsu's relaxation time including bird watching, these inventive thoughts would not have been able to later form the basis of problem solving.

A friend of mine is an ocean sailor. He grew up the son of a naval officer in Portsmouth and the children sailed the channel from early years. Later becoming an orthopaedic surgeon, one day he was using a turnbuckle to put tension into the yacht lines when he had a similar crossover moment.

Although he had not consciously been thinking about the problem of management of post-surgical wound drainage, the solution seemed immediately apparent.

From this crossover moment came a patented surgical turnbuckle to manage healing of orthopaedic wounds.

Similarly, a client of ours uses strain gauges from F1 cars and pulleys from racing yachts in his physiotherapy diagnostic equipment, a component of which helps train F1 drivers to develop their neck muscles to withstand the incredible G forces caused by their cars on the tight circuits at speed. Never has this been more important. At the time of writing, an article by Raphael Orlove reported[49] that in the 2017 Australian Grand Prix, Hamilton pulled 6.5g – up 1.2g from 2016. He says that is the equivalent of adding another one and a fifth body weight to hold up.

Perhaps you and your team can benefit from this sort of cross-over thinking, using examples from your hobbies and interests to problem solving issues affecting the company and its products.

In Stephen Covey's book 'First Things First'[50] there is this gem called:

The first thing is to keep the first thing, the first thing.

In that context, write your 3 and 6 month priorities on the template below.

Print them and keep to one side of your desk or work space so while you are making day to day decisions you have them in your vision. They will help order the rest of your priorities.

As something pressing needs attention you can look at the stated priorities on your short and long term planning sheet and decide if they need to be re-prioritised.

This gives you a benchmark against which to say "Is this new item just pressing and important – or a priority that supersedes previous priorities?"

Today, make a note in your diary **One Month From Now** to re-do your lists, and update each month.

During explosive growth,
keeping track of the priorities is a real challenge.

It's hard to discriminate between
the most pressing,
important,
urgent, or
critical thing to do.

---

[49] www.blackflag.jalopnik.com/see-how-much-more-intense-the-g-forces-are-in-f1snew-c-1793888742100

[50] First Things First. Steven Covey ISBN 0-684-80202-1

In this atmosphere of fast growth things like long and short term planning take on a whole new concept.

Short term is 3 months. Long, is 6!

Fill in the blanks below and keep the list where you can see it.

MOTTO

First Things First

SHORT TERM PRIORITIES

For the next 3 months the 2 priorities are:

ONE

_____

_____

_____

TWO

_____

_____

_____

LONG TERM PRIORITIES

For the next 6 months the 2 priorities are:

ONE

_____

_____

_____

TWO

_____

_____

_____

Check your focus by re-evaluating the mix

- ✓ You've spelled out where you are right now.
- ✓ You've described the company and drawn some conclusions about the sort of environment you are creating.
- ✓ You've described the people we have and worked out who you need next.
- ✓ You've checked that the Management Team all think they work at the same company you do, and when they talk they all describe that same company so the market isn't confused.
- ✓ You've thought about and drafted a plan to help integrate people quickly so they feel they 'own' the company.
- ✓ You know your immediate and longer term priorities.

Before you look back at the work you've already done to this point, it's time to not think for a bit and let your mind do some subconscious sorting.

It's one thing to have all this evolve, as it does when you start up and things start growing around you. It's quite another to take the time to sit down and re-evaluate. But you know it's important. That's why you bought the book, right?

Go and make a cup of tea or coffee. If you are taking some planning time at home, pour a drink, wander around, look at the garden, take the dog for a walk, go for a drive. Not all at once! Just take a short break. Take an hour.

If you are doing this as a group, pile into a couple of vehicles and drive to somewhere nearby you usually don't go – a nearby outdoor space, a park, the pier, a fun fair. Wander around. Check out the sights – but just for an hour.

If it makes you feel decadent, don't. You're working.It's called Walking-Work-Technology: a great concept developed by a colleague of mine from Bologna, Italy, Dr Lilia Infilese[51].

Lilia designed this for groups made up from diverse cultures within the European Union so that they would have an informal break to get to know each other, and discuss agenda items on a one-to-one level before concluding their seminars.

This concept was in turn brought to MOSAICO, which at that time was a group of some of the top Training and Leadership Development professionals in Europe. We used it at each meeting and apart from the pure enjoyment; it has a way of sifting out irrelevancies and highlighting new thoughts on the topics under discussion. The impact of a different environment brings new connections to the issue just by changing the physical surroundings and the expectations of that precious hour.

In the course of these breaks we rambled through the countryside and in small villages. People form informal groups. They talked about the subject at hand: exploring new concepts. Thought processes are broken by new sights, sounds, experiences. People got to know each other in a new context of evaluation.

The results when you re-group are interestingly refreshed, and show more expansive thinking.

Use this time to think about what you have described so far. This is the preparation time for ideas to percolate before drafting your plan. It works. Try it.

It's not just Lilia's idea, it has scientific underpinnings. A University of Michigan article[52] published in Psychiatry Today describes

---

[51] Dr. Lilia Infilese www.artes-research.com

[52]

www.researchgate.net/publication/23718837_The_Cognitive_Benefits_of_Interacting_With_Nature Marc. G. Bergman, John Jonides, and Stephen Kaplan – University of Michigan Published in Psychological Science Dec 1, 2008.

the benefits of walking in nature or viewing pictures of nature to improve directed-attention abilities.

Here is a summary of the findings:

- Attention restoration theory (ART) provides an analysis of the kinds of environments that lead to improvements in directed-attention abilities.
- Nature, which is filled with intriguing stimuli, modestly grabs attention in a bottom-up fashion, allowing top-down directed-attention abilities a chance to replenish.
- Unlike natural environments, urban environments are filled with stimulation that captures attention dramatically and additionally requires directed attention (e.g., to avoid being hit by a car), making them less restorative.

However you describe your company as it operates today, be honest about what works and what doesn't.

You need to design carefully for the future and that begs a valid baseline.

You've grown success well. Keep on doing so.

A complex system that works is invariably found to have evolved from a simple system that worked.

A complex system designed from scratch never works and cannot be patched up to make it work.

You have to start over, beginning with a working simple system.

John Gall[53] - Gall's Law

---

[53] John Gall: General SystemAntics: an essay on how systems work, and especially how they fail. ISBN-10: 0961825103; ISBN-13: 978-0961825102

Chapter Eleven

Getting to 'Wow'. The power of design.

Practice safe design:
Use a concept.

Petrula Vrontikis[54]

What needs to change if you are going to create the company you described? How will it look in two years time?

Draw the plan

To get where we want to be in two years we need to make changes to the following:

Circle any that apply.

Operational Structure
1. Office layout
2. Car parking arrangements
3. Reception and telephone handling
4. Plant layout (Non green things)
5. Plant Operation (Non green things)
6. Operations Manual
7. Induction Program
8. Warehousing
9. Inventory Control
10. Order Processing
11. Mail handling
12. Company vehicles
13. Trade Show attendance
14. Market perception

---

[54] Petrula Vrontikis is a designer, author and educator, based in Los Angeles. In 2003 she was selected by Graphic Design:USA Magazine as one of the 100 designers to watch. Her company is called 35K – which is the amount she received for the original name of the company: VDO.

15. Methods of hiring
16. Plants (green things)
17. Training
18. Review IT system suitability
19. _____

20. _____

21. _____

22. _____

23. _____

24. _____

25. _____

Staff
Existing staff re-organisation

- Address situation of people not performing at previous level
- Rewarding existing staff for efforts to date
- Hiring new staff
- Dress code
- Music at work
- Flexibility of personal work area layout
- Social events
- Company meetings
- Team meetings
- Teams
- Benefits
- Virtual office (on-line access from anywhere)
- Work hours
- Companywide holidays

Organisation days (a day when the department stops operation to physically restructure. This includes a complete review of everything in the files (virtual and otherwise) and throwing out, shredding, ceremonial cremation of everything out dated, superseded or **safe** to throw out. Following along Rule Number 4.)

Rule Number 4:

Virtual filing has a common framework with the right
people having the right access to the right things.

Virtual filing should have a common framework,
with the right people
having the right access to the right things.

One actual under desk filing cabinet per person. One filing cabinet per group. Empty the group one before you can make a case for another.

Under each heading you have circled list the specific things that need to change. Just list them in dot point order. This is your Business Plan outline.

See! Business Planning can be a lot easier than you thought.

Now match the plan outline with an organisational structure that fits the need of the company you have just described.

Design the structure

Fast growth companies need a different structure than the lineal one that is the traditional model.

Get creative. To get you this far, you've been a small cohesive group with a particular personality and culture.

Can you get a few of these working collaboratively in small groups and try and keep the flexibility that has served you so well? You need to do something untraditional because the structured layers familiar to us in big companies are the barriers to enabling the flexibility you need.

At PayPal each person was responsible for and measured against one outcome – just one. This stopped overlap and kept focus. It may work for you.

One easy way to work out a company structure which can even include who gets paid what, is dead easy.

- Write the job title of every job in the company (as it is right now) on a Post It note: one per job title.
- Stick them all on a White Board, all along the left hand side of the board in a neat series of rows.

Don't have a White Board? Use a window. A window with a sheet behind it makes a great White Board. I made this improvisation while doing Marketing Planning with a company in the mountains of Indonesia.

- Now pick any one of the jobs and stick it in the middle of the White Board/window.

- Ask yourself – or your team: "Relative to this job, how does...(and select "any other Post-It title)... relate?

This can help you sort out logical relationships, which in turn can help you to establish who gets paid what in relationship to another. It's time consuming, but it will give you some fair order of reporting requirements and also of how pay levels relate to each other.

It may give insight into how small groups could be formed, and with how they would interact with other small groups, keeping the small company feel despite growing larger.

It's not high sophistication, but it worked for one of Britain's main brewers when they decided to take twenty eight pay scales and merge them into eight! If it can work in an environment of high unionisation, it can certainly work for you. Just an aside: This same company took the current rate of pay including overtime as the baseline of what they would now pay as the basic wage. Then they deducted pay for every hour of overtime worked. Interesting concept.

By doing it this way they protected the wage level to which their employees had become accustomed, but actually gave a good reason why the work practices that required overtime needed improvement.

Employees quickly came up with their own improved work practices to avoid being docked for overtime hours worked. They also helped those less skilled to gain the skills required to be able to complete their bit of the jigsaw whose pieces together made up the overall company picture.

An unexpected side effect was that the person universally thought to be the least able to be skilled, the person who held the job of cleaning out the vats – the lowliest of jobs – taught himself at an accelerated rate once given the chance. He proved to be one of the most productive and upwardly mobile of employees under the new system. Maybe you can release some of the gold on your shop floor.

Now make an organisational chart from your Post It collage and circulate to the whole Management Team with a watermark saying 'Draft' in BIG LETTERS all across it! Do nothing more with this until you re-group in 6 weeks time! Let it percolate!

Everything is designed.
Few things are designed well.

Brian Reed[55]

---

[55] Brian Reed is a successful games designer and developer who also worked on Marvel Comics www.en.wikipedia.org/wiki/Brian_Reed

Chapter Twelve

Marketing without advertising:

Prepare the market

All things being equal,
people will do business with a friend.

All things being unequal,
people will still do business with a friend.

Mark McCormack[56]

What are you going to do to make yourself so madly fascinating that you don't pay to promote yourself, others do it for you?

Let's undertake a few planning activities right now.

Our Learning Module 'Harnessing Your Unpaid Marketing Team' is based on the sort of information you gather here.

Use ours to design yours.

List One - Influencers

Who are your:

- Suppliers
- Competitors
- Colleagues And Friends
- Peers
- Essential Support Infrastructure (Lawyers, Accountants,
- Universities Or Research Institutes, Etc.)
- Influencers In Your Market
- Trade Press

---

[56] Mark McCormack was an American lawyer who founded (IMG), the International Management Group to serve celebrities and sports figures after a career as a sports agent and writer. He was the first to see the potential for endorsements as an income stream. His books include 'What They Don't Teach you at Harvard Business School' and its sequel 'What they STILL Don't...'

- Local Press
- National Press
- International Press
- Local Schools, Colleges, Technical Establishments,
- Research Centres, Art Colleges
- Local Charities what are you passionate about outside of work?

List Two - Interests

Yours: What are you passionate about outside of work?

_____

_____

_____

_____

_____

_____

_____

List Three - Management team interests

What about the rest of the Management Team?
What are their passions outside work?
Let them answer these themselves.
What do they care about, the things they want to contribute some effort to?
Saving the Sabre Toothed Tiger; Model Aeroplanes; Wine; Antique and Classic Cars; Fund-Raising for the local school or the hospice; Fishing; Training Retriever Dogs; Collecting Butterflies, Chinese Vases, Comics, Jazz memorabilia; performing for a band, orchestra, rep theatre, opera, dance group ; dancing: some aspect of sport; improved opportunities for young people?

Each of you make a list.

Then consolidate into one list that relates person to interest

_____

_____

_____

_____

_____

_____

_____

_____

_____

_____

List Four - Issues

In your industry are there any really important issues people focus on? If so, list them.

_____

_____

_____

_____

_____

List Five - Tourism & events

In your region what are the big tourism events and attractions? List.

_____

_____

_____

_____

_____

_____

_____

_____

_____

_____

_____

List Six - Identity

What colour is your corporate livery? You know: the colour of your website, delivery vans, the corporate logo and the image you project? If it does the job you want, or doesn't do the job you want, say why here:

_____

_____

_____

_____

_____

_____

_____

_____

_____

_____

We already know what the company does and what is so special about it that it is causing explosive growth.

Now, all we have to do is work out who can carry the message about how madly fascinating we are to our key targets in the market. Then they can create market curiosity and knowledge about you.

To do so effectively, we need to think through why they'd bother to do this for us: for nothing.

That's the easy part actually. Now you have several lists of potential collaborators. For each one on the list, think why what you do might have meaning for them.

Collaborate:

Would a bit of something you make or supply together with a bit of something they make or supply form a new product: even a silly fun product just made for promotional benefit?

Here are some examples. The first one I know because I was one of the two people that pushed this collaboration through against company preference to stick with an inferior in-house solution that had been slightly improved.

A small fast growth company had refined a bit of their IT transformation to a level much better than that offered as part of a generic own-branded one. A big global corporation found that the weakest link in their IT transformation was the bit this small company did so well.

By collaborating with the smaller company throughout Europe, and using their product packaged within that of the global giant, over a period of less than a year seventy-five new potential clients were directly introduced by the smaller company – and of those fifty-four turned into customers.

As an aside – within two years that same fast growth small company was bought by Cisco Systems.

Here is another example I found in an inspiring report by Teresa Turiera & Susanna Cros[57], on inter-company collaboration that prompted me to investigate further.

Comité Colbert is a collaborative association that brings together seventy-five of the most important French companies from the luxury goods sector to work together on things important to them all. The association has a long history.

Founded in 1954 by the famous fashion designer Jean-Jaques Guerlain to promote the luxury goods of France, it has since grown so that today 86% of their products are exported.

The collaborative seeks input from students of top art schools on their view of the luxury goods market. They choose a theme and then bring together celebrities and other luxury goods purchasers to discuss them, together with the students. This way they always have personal insight in the desires and needs of the future market and can respond accordingly. It also educates young students about the possibilities of employment in traditional fine craftsmanship.

---

[57] Co-Society presents: Co-Business 50 examples of business collaboration: Teresa Turiera &Susanna Cros www.co-society.com/wp-content/uploads/CO_business_2013.pdf

The success of the Comité Colbert has been so notable that their membership now has eighty-one members divided into twelve industry sectors.

Through collaboration, the business of Comité Colbert members has increased fivefold.

Success breeds success and they now also collaborate with like clusters in Spain, Italy, and the UK, setting up the European Cultural and Creative Industries Alliance (ECCIA).

The German luxury goods sector has its own counterpart 'Meisterkreis' which now also collaborates with Comité Colbert.

Collaboration generates business growth for participants faster together than alone.

A good collaborative arrangement may prove to be more than the sum of the parts of each company.

The same report lists the collaboration between NASA and Lego to have astronauts in space use Lego to excite young people to scientific concepts. This collaboration was inspired by the need to improve intake to Science, Technology, Engineering, and Maths courses in schools.

A more familiar example in the UK is that of an oil company and a quality food retailer: BP and Marks & Spencer (M&S). M&S is a UK based multinational store well known over its long history for clothing and home wares, but more recently for high quality food. BP uses the leverage of the popularity of M&S foods to promote itself as 'not just any forecourt'.

The resulting thoughts for your business on collaborative possibilities? List them here:

_____

_____

_____

_____

_____

_____

_____

_____

_____

_____

_____

Tap into the power of your whole wide network

Never was this more relevant than in this era which is dominated by social media.

A very useful insight into this trend is reported in a White Paper by Crowd Tap[58]. It is worth visiting their website to read it, but here are some interesting highlights from the main message which is distilled simply as:

- Get close to your consumers and let them influence the direction of your products.

The paper lists some important findings:

- A consumer today is estimated to be exposed to over 5,000 marketing images.
- Customers who become Brand Advocates (those involved closely with how the brand evolves) spend twice as much as other customers and recommend between two and four times as often as other customers.
- Content involvement does not mean devolving your core offer, it means refining it.

Let's look in detail at your lists about those you can harness in your unpaid marketing team and consider some suggestions for each of them.

As before, these are just suggestions. Your team should have many more. These ideas are just to start the thinking process. Use them if you want, but also create your own.

_____

[58] CrowdTap: The Creative Marketing Future: How co-creation and advocacy will drive winning companies www.corp.crowdtap.com.s3-website-us-east-1.amazonaws.com/whitepapers/Crowdtap-Collaborative-Marketing-Future.pdf

If any of these ideas, or any other aspect of this book for that matter, proves helpful to your business let me know. With your permission, I will promote your business as I publish the results. If you do so, tell me why we all should care about your business and want to promote it.

What's your specialty? I could become part of your unpaid marketing team.

You'll never see the groups of people on your lists the same way in the future.

Through the prism of multifaceted angles where your company's best features are somehow refracted in conjunction with theirs, you'll find they will suggest new forms of relationship.

What to do with what you have discovered about the potential for a good unpaid marketing team from your lists?

Harnessing List One - Influencers
Suppliers

In your own marketing media can you make reference to the difference quality makes and each quarter publish a profile of one of your suppliers?

It's good business. A side benefit may be that since you are promoting your associate company's expertise this creates a different relationship with them.

This may also diffuse any tensions in the sorting out any issues that emerge in your supply chain – because you are now in a relationship other than you and me on opposing sides of the issue – you are now collaborators who can sort things out together with minimal fallout.

It also means that your supplier will circulate this third party reference throughout its network, therefore widening yours.

Competitors

> *Your real competitors are those in the global marketplace.*
> *They are seldom who you think they are.*

In the 1990s a colleague of mine worked with one of the global giants in farm machinery manufacture. He was able to get the companies identified as 'the competition' to share their market share information with his company on the basis that the final report would be available to all who participated. In other words one company was paying to agglomerate the data from them all.

The final report radically changed the focus of every company surveyed. Each was amazed to find that there were one or two particular areas of specialty for their company writ large in the data. Although the other companies were present in that sector of the market, each of them had a very clearly defined niche of the overall market place.

By restructuring to these newly identified strengths they were each able to assist the other's success in the markets divested.

Working with the coffee industry in New Orleans we came to a level of trust where their closely held marketing insights were shared. To their surprise the members of this collaborative cluster found that each had totally different perspectives on a complex market place. Like a kaleidoscope taking fractures of colour, when twisted together, these fragments made a much more meaningful picture from which each company benefited. It enabled a collective plan to be developed to refocus on promoting the specific benefits of the New Orleans coffee business.

Instead of instinctively 'feeling' that claims made by competitive ports and centres of coffee packaging and distribution were ill based in fact, they now had real data that provided inarguable facts that influenced buying decisions of the potential clients of each of those who had shared their data.

Is it possible the same holds for your company? Take a careful look at the companies you see as competitors and make a new evaluation of their strengths vs. yours.

Now are your competitors who you thought they were?

Is it possible to find a common theme on which you can join with competitors on the same speaking platform and host this event yourselves? It will expose you to their clients and their networks as they promote it – and of course them to yours. But if you have already done your evaluation, this might be profitable for each of you - a classic Win:Win.

Does it make sense to collaborate on some known industry-wide issue that is constraining everyone's business?

The port of Cairns in tropical north Queensland, Australia, had a wide variety of yacht servicing businesses, just as one would reasonably expect from a port in paradise. Until they came together as a group, they hadn't been able to identify where working together would increase the business of each of them.

Once they identified the wide range of skills already well-developed and individually holding a great reputation in the industry, the group clustered these as a Super Yacht Servicing group and went off to the Fort Lauderdale Boat Show. They came back with orders in their millions – and the Port Authority, which had plans to extend the harbour ten years hence, realised the potential and brought construction forward to start in three years time.

Give some thoughts to how you can bring your competition together to develop a consortium that helps each business. The combination of what you do, plus what the companies you now see as competitors do, may bring the sorts of profits that will make all ships rise.

Colleagues and friends

Never was the point about how this also applies to colleagues and friends made more clearly than one gorgeous summer day when I was sailing in the Whitsundays on the Great Barrier Reef in Australia with some friends and colleagues. We were working in a fast growing Recruitment Company where I was on a short contract helping them draw seven fiercely independent branches into one cohesive organisation.

The yacht owners were architects. They were chatting together about their new hires who were to start the following month – and wondering aloud if they were potential crew for the yacht in the racing season.

The young professional of about 30 who had sailed with them since her teens stared at them in disbelief. She said in puzzlement: "You hired two new architects?" When answered in the affirmative, she asked why they hadn't done so through her. In surprise the yacht owners replied that they thought she just dealt with temps. When she first started at the company she did. That was almost 10 years ago.

She lost the fees associated with those two professional placements simply because she hadn't updated her friends on what skills she had developed and now had to offer.

Don't assume that people you know have kept up with progress of your fast growth company, and you. At my own expense I learned the corollary to this: make sure you know what your colleagues and peers are actually doing now. What has changed since when you last understood what they do?

I had early agreement to be the lead on a major project across the whole of Europe but the client needed to restructure and refine the product.

Knowing the original timetable for this I didn't keep touch as regularly as would have been wise. When I reconnected that progress had been faster than planned and - someone else had claimed continental Europe. I ended up with the UK: a nice market but...

Peers

In working with leaders in the petrochemical industry in New Orleans I saw the perfect example of how this can work with peers.

These business leaders had gathered to develop a strategy for the sector that would benefit each company in its own way by improving the overall environment in which they operated.

These were well-qualified people who knew their industry. Naturally each was well-aware of the fellow companies within the industry and therefore felt they knew what they produced. For years these same men had met at seminars, conferences and sat together on committees.

On one occasion one of them was late for one of our meetings and apologised as he sat down, explaining that the plant had just finished a rather challenging production run from which there was a by-product that was hard to sell as it had a limited market, but needed to be removed from site quickly.

Sitting next to him was a colleague from another company who drew back his chair in amazement. With no knowledge that this by-product was being manufactured at the plant next to him, and it being an important component in a chemical mixture of their own, his company was shipping raw material in down the whole length of the Mississippi River when they could get it from next door.

In a similar situation, for over two years, as Executive Director of a Regional Development Association, I reported to a Board. On this Board a colleague in a similar field to my own represented his sub-regional organisation. I was leaving that role and before doing so had cause to visit him in his own office, something that hadn't taken place before because we had met only at Board Meetings and official functions. On the wall were certificates announcing his studies in Hospital and Health Care Management.

In the role I was just leaving we had previously had occasion to need specialist advice in hospital management. It had been hard to come by and expensive. It was advice that I could have gained through just asking my colleague had I but known that his current job saw him working outside the field of his original credentials. It shouldn't be surprising.

Reports show varying numbers – all over 50% –of graduates work outside their field of University study.

A LinkedIn based study related in Forbes in 2015[59] tracked the movement of graduate talent to Silicon Valley and San Francisco.

---

[59] Forbes Aug 17,2015 George Anders: That 'Useless'' Liberal Arts Degree Has Become Tech's Hottest Ticket.www.forbes.com/sites/georgeanders/2015/07/29/liberal-arts-degree-tech/#3ef8f280745d

The study found that only 30% were in engineering or coding. Sales and marketing accounted for 14%, while 6% went into education and training, 5% into consulting and 5% into business development. The rest were dispersed in diverse fields such as Real Estate and Product Management.

Code writers often hold in awe the Liberal Arts graduates who can liaise with clients to figure out what they really want and then translate that into simple specifications.

This begs two questions:

1. Do your peers know precisely what you do, and you what they do?
2. If it is a known fact that most people work outside their field of original study - are you hiring practices falsely skewed to holders of degrees and other credentials that actually give little prediction of likely ability to do the job?

Former Editor of WIRED Magazine Chris Anderson looked at all the contributors to his Open Source Drone project to find the best person to start his drone business.

Jordi Muñoz was the person he selected because of his great track record of problem solving. Tasked with developing the company and with just a few hundred dollars funding from Chris's own pocket, Muñoz developed the whole business until it got so large it needed what any modern manufacturing facility needs, and these too he effected when the factory moved to Tijuana.

When selected, Muñoz was then an unemployed Mexican waiting for his Green Card to allow him to work in the US. He spent the time available from not being employed to hone skills in an area of interest. Being fascinated with this emerging drone technology and it being too new for there to be much information, he taught himself.

Remember what we discussed about Temp Workers? The Muñoz story illustrates the reality of where talent can be found in this era.

There is an incredible pool of talent
in the University of the Future,
where people teach themselves.

These students come with proof of ability.

They may not have a certificate or diploma or degree that you recognise and they may never graduate. That's because they have such a passion for learning they keep on advancing their skills.

Shouldn't you be looking to this 'University Without Walls' for talent for your business? Or are you still selecting applicants based upon Key Word searches in CVs?

There is an onward cautionary note from this story. According to a Forbes report by Ryan Mac[60], 3D Robotics has since failed after rapid growth.

Just because you are first in the market
doesn't mean you can hold the lead position.

Brutal price slashing from Chinese Drone Company DJI and emergence of a flock of burgeoning Chinese drone manufacturers, plus all sorts of problems in developing and marketing the 3D Robotics product has led to the demise of the company. It now has a sole focus on enterprise software.

Professional support infrastructure

This is made up of people like: Lawyers, Accountants, Investors, Bankers, Universities or Research Institutes, etc. The professionals who give you advice in the management of your legal and financial affairs are a great resource to tap into for promoting your business.

Have you ever thought of offering talks on some aspect of your business that your law or accountancy firm or bank can host for their clients? These talks need to inform potential clients about something relevant about which they knew little or nothing at all – and not be just a self promo effort.

Is there some more R&D needed to refine your business or its processes? Your local University or research institute can partner with you to develop this – and promote your business to the international academic community along the way.

What sort of communication do you have with your investors? You should be managing this. It's a lot harder to get new ones than tap the ones you already have and get connected to their networks of like investors.

Don't make whatever form of investor communication you choose be boring and predictable. Create something with pizzazz but not trying hard to be clever or smart – and don't make it too costly – or they'll

---

[60] Forbes Oct 5 2016 Ryan Mac: Behind the Crash of 3D Robotics, North America's Most Promising Drone Company www.forbes.com/sites/ryanmac/2016/10/05/3d-robotics-solo-crash-chris-anderson/#c2adc063ff5b

wonder why you are spending valuable funds on marketing materials for them.

Can you send them a half yearly something that is a part of your company? It might be a component part of a new product, a jar of jelly beans that is filled with the same number of jelly beans as the number of clients you had this year. You might even colour code the jelly beans for types of client by longevity or volume of purchase, or type of industry sector.

In either of the cases suggested, the part or the jar of jelly beans is likely to sit on the Investor's desk and keep on selling to those visiting your Investor's office.

Make sure whatever you do goes to an office address so that it can keep on promoting you to everyone who comments on it. Get your teams together and think of something creative.

Influencers in your market

Danny Brown and Sam Fiorella of Sensei Marketing[61] in their book 'Influence Marketing' use research to demonstrate how to work with influencers. Here, they make the distinction between 'macro-influencers' and 'micro-influencers'.

For your purposes, the person who has a smaller reach but whose impact is highly respected might be the relationship you want to develop. Knowing who they are means you are in tune with your market and how it operates, who has the insight that others take cues from, etc.

CC Group, a London B2B technology PR agency, outlines what you need to know about the influencer before developing that relationship. You need to evaluate:

- What form of communication is used
- What the motivation is for wanting to be an influencer (writing a book, doing research, building a business, etc)
- What is the particular section of your market that sparks his or her interest?

Then your job is to show how your products or services are useful.

Like any good relationship, working with an Influencer
is not a one-off effort but something that continues.

---

[61] Danny Brown and Sam Fiorella: Influence Marketing: How to Create, Manage and Measure Brand ISBN-10: 0789751046; ISBN-13: 978-0789751041

The media
Local, national and international press

Reporters and journalists are usually scrambling to meet deadlines and to find fresh information that is credible, newsworthy, thought provoking, or entertaining (or a mixture of these) and that has relevance to their audience.

They are also generally thought to be cynical and tightly focused on a snappy version of any story. In that context think about potential to develop that relationship.

Making yourself credible in the media can attract new clients and position your company with higher credibility.

Who is your media spokesperson?

There should be just one in the company. If he or she is not currently comfortable in being interviewed on TV – make the investment in a short course. As you grow, you may find it the best investment you ever made –especially if the spokesperson is you! The spokesperson should use his or her own way of explaining things.

That's why you choose carefully, because what is said should reflect the topic clearly, but when said genuinely and not as a script will be more believable.

Do you have a Media Schedule?

This is quite literally a forward plan of what promotion you will do, when, where and at what cost. Even a small company should have one.

All forms of promotion are a black art. We know some of it works – but which bit, at what time, and how?

If we understood that better, we would benefit more directly from our marketing efforts.

Rightly said

A word of warning: see all copy before print!

Please check grammar.

The English Department and International Student Department of a highly reputable UK College in a well known and iconic English city were horrified when posters on buses and poster boards around the region proclaimed a college event with 'More history, less Romans'.

This is a school that has a robust business in teaching English as a second language to students from all over the world. They have built their reputation on sound principles and good teaching of English.

Making the grammatical error of 'Less' Romans instead of 'Fewer' Romans was bad enough, but proclaiming it on buses and bill boards was a disaster. It contradicted everything they had built. When challenged, the person who signed it off (and had not had the English Department check it) said that it had cost a lot so should stay. The real cost was far greater.

This was a classic case of unverified text being used for external promotion. That is why you need to have some checks in place to protect the reputation you have built from being damaged by a simple oversight within a widely promoted and otherwise innocent document or advertisement.

When is an apostrophe not an apostrophe?

When it is a 'prophet' of sloppiness in editing.

Please have someone in charge of apostrophes!

Things like the plural of an acronym need no apostrophe. Not every 'Its' needs an apostrophe. Plurals in general need no apostrophe unless they are possessive – that means they relate to something/someone else: the Club's records – Sarah's book.

Professionalism should sit at the heart of everything you do.

I was asked to review a company in Cambridge for suitability for a client of ours. The website was a case study in appalling grammar. Their claims to have worked for some Cambridge luminaries whose own cachet was global and untarnished were made totally implausible by their total lack of professional use of the language on their website. Despite having heard of some of their successes, I couldn't afford to recommend them.

I spoke to the person who had referred me to it as an Influencer in the industry.

She investigated and told me the senior management used a marketing company to do their website.

Remember what we said about outsourcing?

The company delivering an outsourced activity
may have the Responsibility to deliver the task,
but you have the Accountability to
ensure it doesn't tarnish your brand in doing so.

How and when and where you place your company media insertions – be they articles, thought pieces, blogs, speaking engagements, trade show appearances and attendances, advertisements – too often depends upon ill-considered and /or spontaneous decisions.

The Media Schedule should depend upon the:

- *Nature of your products or services and the nature of your sales cycle:* Does severe weather mean a boom in sales – or new space mission announcements – or reports on a shortage of cocoa next year – or new regulations or laws.
- *Product lifecycle:* Are your products new to an existing market; creating a new market (and if so for buyers in which sectors of business or industry?); mature and capitalising on reputation and success; or in decline and seeking new partnerships and collaborations to reinvigorate them?
- *Existing pattern of your chosen marketplace:* Must you be ready for the Paris or London Fashion Weeks, the Abu Dhabi International Petroleum Exhibition and Conference (ADIPEC), the ITB World leading Travel Show in Berlin, the Chicago Auto Show, Farnborough Air Show in England, E3 in Los Angeles for Interactive Media, *gamescom* in Cologne?

  Whatever your field, you should know the place and time when those who have a focus on your industry gather together – and plan to be there – but not without careful planning far enough ahead.

  Make sure all the complementary media, documentation and staff availability and training is undertaken so the high cost of involvement or attendance brings measurable results.
- *Availability of your resources to maintain the actions it plans –* and the people and funds needed.
- *Need to respond to changes in your market place by a new entrant with a competitive product –* or a complementary product, or by a black swan – something that no one could have predicted but which changes the perception of what was previously accepted as fact.

Trade press

The trade press is usually respected as providing quality and relatively impartial informative content. If you have White Papers or thought pieces or Case Studies illustrating why you have something others in your industry can benefit from, this is a great way to harness valuable third party focus.

Local Press

Don't under-estimate the power of your local press and free dailies. Despite what we read about the decline of print media, the small local newspaper seems to still keep dropping through letterboxes. It is usually read by at least one member of the household – and the local newspapers often seek stories of local success. That's you!

National Press

Usually, the national press place news about your business in comparison to something else that has a place in the national consciousness. It's worth you defining the context before they do.

> *When dealing with the press choose your own platform.*
> *If the national press wants to move you to another,*
> *just keep bouncing back to the one you choose.*

> *If you haven't defined it beforehand*
> *you may end up where you don't want to be.*

International Press

In 1998 an article appeared in the British Airways Business Life Magazine[62] that demonstrates the power of harnessing the international press.

An article by Donnie Morrison offered specific business opportunities to companies seeking high quality workers and showed why hiring a highly motivated virtual workforce based in the Outer Hebrides in the Western Isles of Scotland made good business sense.

Donnie cited specialist thinking skills harnessing IT to deliver quality output to an international and diverse client base and spoke into existence the employment boom that followed.

The contracts that ensued saw steady and increasing growth in engagement of the islands' workforce and accelerated their up-skilling to become a highly savvy and computer literate workforce.

> *The right article at the right time in the right place*
> *to attract the right audience:*
> *sometimes the stars are aligned in your favour.*

---

[62] http://www.work-global.com/news/index.php?id=1

I am privileged to know Donnie and almost moved to the island of Lewis in 2002, attracted by its wild beauty and despite beliefs to the contrary within Britain, a surprisingly good climate tempered by the Gulf Stream.

I couldn't afford to now. It is an economy rebuilt and a desirable destination for those whose work is location agnostic. The economy has found a robust future because of the efforts of one catalyst for growth and his love of the region, his ability to build early small successes based on a global outlook, and harnessing an in-flight executive audience.

Local schools, colleges, technical establishments, research centres, art colleges.

Here are three good reasons to work out how to engage the educational establishments of your area in aspects of your business.

- Students have parents and their parents have friends.
- You'll be looking for talent as you grow.
- You care about your local community.

Gene Haas is best known internationally for his success as owner of the Haas F1 Team. Haas also collaborates with Vincennes University in Indiana. The Haas CNC machines populate an award winning training centre at the university. Students and teachers from all over the USA learn how to use the equipment. The students learn hands on first before being allowed to use computers to implement precision machine tool work. This is a win:win for the company and for the future users of their machinery.

Apple donated computers to school districts in the early days of PCs because they realised that they needed to have the kids become familiar with a totally new technology through using Apple computers instead of the IBM PC of their Dad.

- Perhaps your links are based on collaborative research – with the academic mark giving your own research and products another form of credibility.
- Perhaps you hold competitions that lead to new solutions or designs –and find you the talent from the 'University of Passionate Learning' we spoke of earlier.
- Maybe you use the college art department in packaging design.

The potential for collaboration with mutual benefit is only limited by your creativity.

Local Charities

If you do something for charity – do something for charity.

*In other words, the benefit you gain from publicity
should be a long way down the list of the reasons for doing it.*

Your own team are best advisors here. They know what charities locally they want to support. You probably do too.

If you don't have any idea, the local Hospice is always a good choice. Someone you love or even you might need it someday.

*If 'Plan A' fails
there are twenty-five other letters in the alphabet.*

Anon

Chapter Thirteen

The Turbo:Topple Point

When the need for operational investment
meets the reality of available cash

If money is your hope for independence
you will never have it.

The only real security that a man will have in this world
is a reserve of knowledge, experience, and ability.

Henry Ford[63]

If you are exploding in growth, someday soon you are going to arrive at an inevitable junction point. I call it the Turbo:Topple Point.

It is a really good idea to have some idea that there is such a thing as the Turbo:Topple Point and to plan for it **before** you get there.

The Turbo:Topple Point
is that cross-over point on the graph where
the growth curve going up,
meets the available funds curve, going down.

Result? Crash and Burn, or engage turbo-charge.

'Crash and Burn' will be the excruciating choice that will be made for you if you can't access the development funds you need fast enough, or if you really have lost either focus on your product and its place in the marketplace, or of disruption in your marketplace – or both.

All of the things we've done so far have helped you in this. The markets will know more about you from word-of-mouth (that finest source of trusted information). The widest range of your colleagues, support and supply infrastructure, local schools, colleges and universities - will all know about your company. You have prepared the market to know the product side.

---

[63] Henry Ford transformed an expensive play toy of the elite into a practical workhorse for the common man in introducing the Model T Ford. To do so he introduced mass production – and combined it with high worker pay.

In our one day Professional Learning Course 'Harnessing your Unpaid Marketing Team' we go into some detail about Socially Responsible Investment Funds. These SRI funds have a limited source of qualifying companies. You should do the same.

OK. You're not listed on the Stock Exchange. But people who make SRI decisions in their investments might well be predisposed to investing in smaller companies that are based on the SRI principles of returning profits and reinvestment for the company, to the community, and to the environment: triple bottom line.

It may be that you decided that you don't want to waltz to the tune of the markets and the opinion of an investor. If not an investor per se, the bank will want to have confidence enough to lend.

Find out what would get you on those lists. Not big enough?

Should you act as if you are and use the same criteria when speaking to your investors whomever they are?

Will it help when you become a publicly listed company?

Should you start the Small and Medium Enterprise SRI Fund? Someone should.

> *Many investors are ready to invest in the good guys.*
> *Aren't you the good guys?*

Work out how your interests and passions can tie into your company efforts.

Keep it honest. After all this is about ethical investment: Yours, as a company, and theirs, as investors.

Issues

In your industry, what are the really important issues people focus on?

Is there anything that your company is doing by its structure, ethics, products, services, staffing policies, that merits attention relative to these issues?

If so – shouldn't you get in contact with the press and let them know? A phone call to one of the people whose names are synonymous with the issues – or an email or Tweet – should do the job.

Or is your company the one that is raising the issues? Better still!

If not, could you be?
Should you be?

Before you travel that track think through the potential drain on your already limited resources and then think again. It's a good thing to do – *but only if it doesn't impact on The First Thing.*

Tourism and events

What are the big tourism events and attractions in your region?

Is there something about your company that can benefit the regional tourism activities?

Would a display of the computer controlled Formula One race car carrying trailers you make help promote the Formula One race to come?

Can you provide the sound speaker systems from your new range to help the local Jazz Festival?

Where is the mix that can help get your name out there? Look at the events of your region: the fairs, the festivals, the tourism icons. What can what you do contribute to an event or to tourism for your area and every area where you have offices?

Identity

What colours are your corporate livery? Have you heard of John Deere Green? Easy Jet Orange? IBM's Big Blue, UPS Brown, Schiaparelli pink or the ubiquitous McDonald's Golden Arches?

What colour is the packaging on Colgate Toothpaste, WD-40, Shell Oil, BP, the tin of Nivea cream, the Coca Cola label?

Is there an identity in how you package yourself that can go into the everyday vocabulary of the masses like this? If not, maybe you could consider it.

Before we leave this all important subject of training our Unpaid Marketing Team...

Press Management in challenging times

When you arrive at the Turbo:Topple Point how are you going to manage your press?

What do I mean?

Well, you have been exploding in growth haven't you?

You are so madly fascinating in what the company is doing that you are on everyone's lips. You've been at full speed with activity and go-ahead signs: new staff, big supply orders... then... this fast fish streaking the frothy
breakers to ride the waves of change - is no longer visible.

Is this fast fish caught in the thunder of the pounding breakers as they crash on shore, or still riding the inner curve, carving an arc of careful angle through the turbulence to emerge perfectly poised?

That is what is now in everyone's thinking as things seem to be slowing down. Remember the options once you reach the Turbo:Topple Point: Crash and Burn, or engage turbocharger?

We've seen how the markets smell blood and initiate a feeding frenzy. We've watched the demise of perfectly good companies who were unprepared for that unexpected focus on their faltering progress. But that is not us! We knew we would reach here right from the start – and we planned for it.

We're not going to be vulnerable to letting others interpret your company position and throw you to the sharks. We've already trained our most important players of the Unpaid Marketing Team – and now they are going to tell our story. It's the story of skill and careful balance. That same skill and balance is a defining factor of market leaders, and guides them through a maelstrom to become survivors of the worst forces the market can create.

So – what is that story?

Simple and effective and plausible, one version goes like this: *(adapt it if it's useful):*

The Shrapnel Free Company has been exploding in growth and we all know the hazards of that.

Things can get out of control while you grow a company that fast. So every now and then you must pick an end point and say:
"We need to stop growth for a brief while and consolidate our existing structure. We need to make sure we're building on all our sound business practices and not overlooking any of the things that have made us successful.

We don't want to stop servicing our existing customers at the level they expect while we overstretch to develop new ones.

We need to stop growing until we are satisfied that we all know what the company looks like today, because it's not the company it was 6 months ago – or even 3 months ago.

We need to adjust our shape and make sure the way we are doing things still fits client needs.

We want to last. We want to ride the waves of growth and change to emerge to take the surfers' crown. So, stick with us while we stop to take stock and plan to manage the next stage of growth.

We want to serve our customers and their emerging needs and need to be sure we are still doing that.

It's true. Isn't it?

You do have to stop growing. You need a cash injection from bank or investor(s) to get to the next stage. Until you regroup you **have** to stop growing.

So you may as well use the time just as you have said in the story above!

But the point is that this will carve you out from those other flashy board riders on the waves of market change.

Don't rely on No Guts:No Glory panache.

Have style enough to be the lead rider
and intend to stay that way
by studying how the waves fall across your surf board
to keep standing when others are dragged under.

You have just told the market something very different than what they would have told others about this sudden change in the pace of activity within your company.

In the absence of your statement they would have drawn other conclusions. One of them would have been that you had reached the Turbo:Topple Point and were on the edge of Crash and Burn.

In fact, they could have pushed you to Crash and Burn by alerting the market that you were vulnerable. But now they know you are sensible in planning to sustain in a fast moving current.

How will they know? Who will tell them?

Your Unpaid Marketing Team.
Who are...?

The recruitment agencies you have taken time to educate about the company by dealing with them as professionals and weeding out those who are not so professional. After all, who do they deal with? Your competitors and your customers: all the people who hire the same sort of people as you do. This infers that they are somehow in your market place.

You want them to tell your story and not one they create in the absence of any comment from you.

Your suppliers and support infrastructure. They will see a sudden drop in expenditure and draw their own conclusions – and talk about it.

Give them your story to tell.
Don't let them create their own.

Your own staff. Have you ever talked to a cab driver about what people talk about in the cab? Many people cab-share en route to work in busy metropolitan areas. You would be amazed at what cabbies have told me about companies with whom I have been engaged to work for a brief period. They tell me what the staff really thinks about the company because they hear unguarded conversations.

Surely you have been out at a restaurant or having a cup of coffee or a drink at the pub and heard people talking about their work, their boss, the attitudes of the work place.

How many times have they said the name of the person, the company, or told things that would make the company leadership cringe if they heard them?

What are the messages your team is sending
about where they work?

Are your own staff likely to tell everyone there that you're about to Crash and Burn? For they surely will if they realise you're at the Turbo:Topple Point before you give them a decent explanation for the sudden slow down. They'll presume that 'Crash and Burn' is the only option unless you have given them reason to believe otherwise – and I don't mean lies either.

I mean reasons.

The best reason is that they just believe in the place so much that they can't conceive of it doing anything but go on into turbo-charge. But they need reassurance that you are headed there by careful, shrapnel-free growth.

If your staff are not having fun, not involved in the forward planning, don't feel comfortable enough to tell you when you start inadvertently laying land mines – then they may be the fastest doomsayers you could ever imagine.

Who will the market believe most?
Exactly.
So make sure they're believers.
Then use this time to do just exactly as your story says.

You have no need to actually tell the people outside the Management Team – and then just those at Executive level, that you are at the Turbo:Topple Point, but you do need to explain credibly to all staff that there is an eye in the hurricane of growth and explain how you plan for them all to emerge unscathed.

*Your Unpaid Marketing Team
is even more important
than one you pay.*

*Their information is considered far more reliable
than that of anyone on your payroll.*

Train them well, treat them fairly,
promote their personal endeavours when you can,
and let them know you appreciate
them in their day jobs outside of their other one
as part of your Unpaid Marketing Team.

Hire the people

We've already talked about this to some extent.

In our One Day Professional Learning Course Fit: 'Hire People Not Skills' we go into detail on how you can prepare to do the best interviews with the minimal time investment, and be able to verify why you made the decisions you did. The main reason we go through the exercise at the outset is to identify the sorts of people who thrive in explosive growth.

You can do this yourself.

Your bamboo scaffolding works best when the people you hire can operate in an arena where the rules are that there are no rules, except for the few cardinal ones you agree with your staff. Most of these should be based on using common sense and not tampering with things that can fall apart if fiddled with.

This means that you need an unusual mix, yet all the people will have one thing in common: change is their natural habitat – or a habitat which excites and inspires them, rather than daunting and intimidating them.

They'll be people who don't thrive in tightly structured organisations but know the invisible boundaries over which it is never wise to wander when operating without that type of structure.

They'll be people who find the opportunity for self-definition exhilarating and heady stuff.

They'll people who respond to your expectation that they have a sense of occasion.

For you, this sort of environment may be the norm. For many people it makes them reel from the lack of constancy – the whole freewheeling feel of it. One of my support staff once told me that sometimes she felt almost physically sick when working in this atmosphere. The way she expressed it was that we changed subjects so many times in a day dealing with competing agendas at a fast pace that it disoriented her.

For people like this it's like having had too much to drink and the room spinning round the bed on which they're lying. They can't spend all day with one foot dropped out of the bed touching the floor to stop the room from spinning: because the pace doesn't stop.

So be careful that your new-comers have an attitude towards change that makes it fun. This may not be immediate, but people adapt and if you make it safe for them to tell you – or their team leaders – that they are struggling with all this self-definition and rapid change of subject, they can be given a slower environment in which to adapt more comfortably.

But don't limit yourself to those who know change already. We all started somewhere and some people coming from rigid and ponderous big companies take a while to adjust to the heady atmosphere of the heights you are pushing to, but they relished it once they acclimatised.

With company 'fit' but not a whole lot of experience at living with rapid change, it is remarkable how adaptive people become.

Often exploding-growth companies need multi-skilled people. It may mean that you need people with a mix of business specific knowledge and expertise of a certain kind pertinent to your product or service.

This was the situation we faced when our growth was threatening shrapnel. Instead of chasing the few individuals who had these unique skill mixes – definitely rare breeds - we isolated the skills into two types: technical and business.

We worked on a simple principle. What you need in explosive growth is to combine people of different skill sets so that at any given time, two of them make one fine person – with precisely the skill mix you need at that time.

The trick is to hire people who can work with ever changing alter-egos. What happens when you do this is that your staff become increasingly cross-skilled as they work with and share the experience of first one person and then another.

Another important point to consider is how you decide on the necessary credentials a person must have for the jobs you need doing.

We needed people with actuarial skills. Almost by definition the average actuary is not the type of person to thrive in an explosive growth environment.

We sought instead what I called 'failed actuaries'.

These were people who had the skills and aptitude for the role of actuary, but couldn't stand the environment because it was too staid and predictable and serious for them. They left the profession – either while still in training or shortly after graduating. Usually it was before.

These were the people who made perfect transmitters of information between our company (where they felt quite at home) and the actuaries (whose tribe they had once visited and so knew the quirks of protocol and sensitivity and could communicate in the tribal language).

Similarly, I once saw a brilliant man repositioned from where he was working as a teacher and getting paid lower than what was the then poverty level to support his family of two children. He became a member of the sales team of a major pharmaceuticals company. Although he had a

PhD in pharmacy, he'd never worked in pharmaceuticals. Instead, he'd run his own business and lost it through poor accounting advice. (With the preparation you are making with the assistance of this book, this won't be you!) .

The teaching job was all he could secure following the closure of his business. As a teacher in the early days of satellite launches, he'd made satellite receiving stations for the children in his school class.

When I asked how he did that, he looked at me in a puzzled way, answering in a rather bemused tone "With their PC". His tone suggested "Doesn't everyone?"

Consider that said PC was one of the very first PCs on the market back in the early 1980's.

He was a person who had the right background for work in a pharmaceutical company, but his other work and life experiences showed that he was a person of wide ranging interests and adaptability and with a practical bent. His new job recognised the interesting mix of these skills and how useful he would be in translating between business person and scientist.

Quickly this chap became a key member of their team, able to understand the technical details and intricate pharmaceutical niceties of high level drugs, yet able to communicate them to medical staff and researchers alike with blinding clarity. He had demonstrated through unrelated activities that he might be a PhD tracking messages from space but he had his feet well placed on the ground.

When hiring for explosive growth companies, look at fit from attitudes displayed in diverse environments at least equally - and we suggest, more as a priority - than the actual developed skills you need.

Introduce the people

Now you have hired new people, how do they come into the team that is already there?

If you tell me they just arrive and one of your staff helps them settle in you're telling me you like shrapnel. Just as well too.

If this is how you see the start of a new team member, let me suggest a few perspectives on this.

You have carefully selected people who thrive in a minimum rules environment. They should be able to get on with it. Right?

Right! As long as they have sufficient information about the whole context in which they have to make their own decisions and 'get on with it'.

Given a 'Come on in – it's over to you' scenario, the person will do the best they can with the information to hand: which is not a lot.

Since their decision-making will be based on a premise for which they have no actual basis in fact, get ready for friendly-fire. Unwittingly, they will make some colossal errors of judgement because you did not give them the proper context within which they could make a good decision. So it would be preferable to set the context with some sort of induction.

"But," you tell me, "We're all too busy to trot around doing Induction Programs."

I know. That's why you bought the book – to find an easier way to achieve the same result – to do the minimum to achieve the maximum result.

What if you prepare – once – an Induction Program?Our One Day Professional Learning Course 'Come On In' works with you to prepare one, but you can do it yourself. Adapt some of our methods to suit your company. Ask the latest people to join the company to help. They've been there and know from the experience what was missing.

An Induction Program needs to be tailored to suit your company. Not by you personally, though you may want to select from the list below regarding content and maybe add some other things to the list. Someone else in the company can do the draft. Once it is prepared for you, what's going to happen?

Oh! You anticipated the answer! You're getting these fun-lunches down pat aren't you? Have the rest of staff go through it at lunch and make irreverent comments and good suggestions.

Is anyone a good amateur cartoonist? Pay them for some good ones that match the text.

There are a few reasons for this method being suggested. Apart from the fact that each of your existing staff has started as a fresh new face in the company and experienced some level of difficulty in 'fitting in' and will therefore be well placed to make sure others have a better experience, there is another reason.

Given the opportunity, your current staff may reveal some interesting burrs under their saddles that you didn't know about. Providing a safe and non-punitive environment to shoot down existing methods of handling things is a great way to let off the steam that frustration at the current system may be generating. They may say you don't need a certain part of the induction because you should scrap a whole process that they have seen as counter-productive.

Remember we commented that Business Planning sometimes comes in unexpected formats? This is one.

Listen carefully to what is said and what is not said, and also to what is inferred during these lunches...but make absolutely sure that you keep the atmosphere light and fun filled if you are serious about getting input that you can use.

> Listen rather than speak.
> Don't get defensive!

The Induction Program should include (as relevant):
- Welcome booklet (available in online version as well to be bookmarked for quick access if needed) with the few rules and the Company Benefits in it plus an outline of any particular Corporate Calendar you may have with special holidays, trade shows, quarterly meetings etc.
- An Emergency Contact Information Form to be completed
- Payroll information
- An Operations Manual about how to do the things that universally require some sort of common format or approach (including copies of all company standard formats for document presentation)
- A personal introduction to relevant people and general introduction around the company departments or groups
- Lunch with pre-assigned colleague(s) for the first three days
- After a few weeks of working there, the program about which we have already spoken to make them feel they own the company – the 'Meet The Management' event.

So let's have a look at a pick-list for the Welcome Book.

Welcome to the Company

This small booklet serves as the unchanging constant – at least for a few months, or until people suggest something better, or you need to present a different image. Therefore, it should be designed to have nothing within it that needs to change for the next six months at least.

How many do you need to print? Do you need to print? Yes – even though there will be an online version as well.

The printed booklet will go home to educate your unpaid workforce. It will sit on the desk, in the car, be browsed by the family and maybe friends curious about 'the new job'. Think of it as is a marketing document as well as an instructional one.

Organise a print-on-demand arrangement. Print the first twenty copies and 'top up' as needed. You may even be able to print them yourselves.

Weigh up the cost: benefit ratio of these options. Don't stint on quality. This is advertising your company to its most important people – yours: your staff and your unpaid marketing team.

The finished product needs to look smart enough to show you are proud of the company and not necessarily be a flash, heavy-duty printing job. However, it does need to be printed on quality paper, be properly edited, and checked by at least three people for spelling and grammatical errors: after all, it's an introduction to your company. You want it to be professional and not a Mickey Mouse version, although even Mickey was literate.

Remember that this is a publication that may be casually strewn about in the employee's home and be read by who knows who. Write it so you'd be proud for your ideal client to read it and that if she did she would be impressed. It needs to reflect the character of the place and the company ethos. If this is formal then so should be the Welcome Booklet. If informal and colourful, the booklet should reflect this.

Instead of the usual predictable letter from you, the Chief PooBah, what about something different?

A one page collage containing a short welcome by you and comments on the company and what people feel about it – from a few different perspectives?

"It's a madhouse but fun!" - Design Team.
"Wait for one of our lunches!" - Warehousing.

Ask the team what would make the best **first image**. Think of some options. Remember to keep it in the style of the company and not be glib or too clever. Creativity needs to be moderated by good judgement and by legal correctness.

Maybe you could include a CD of music of a local musician or band (possibly that to which a staff member belongs), purchased and re-labelled with your corporate livery. Remember that you asked your staff about their interests. Surely the answers to that may lead you to the right source.

You could have a series of these for a small investment. They could be your client promotional gifts at Christmas - jazz, folk, instrumental, classics. Remember to ensure all the copyright is securely addressed so your local artists are protected.

Or is there a company T-Shirt? Hat? Pen? As well as the CD? Instead of? The T-Shirt, hat, pen are nice. They've all been done before by others. They are done for the same sound reason: to make people feel they're welcome and part of the team. They also offer free promotion when used or worn.

Some more personal tribute like the CD can be a point of difference and give you a new group on your Unpaid Marketing Team - the musicians in your community. Pay them fairly and make sure they know what the company sells and why it's special so they can comply with Rule Number 1. You may even have them perform at your 'Introduction to the Company' or other corporate events.

It helps your triple bottom line approach of supporting your community; it is not usual; it's certainly a welcoming gesture; and it is memorable –remember Rule number 1?

> Rule Number 1.
> Everyone IN the company
> is potentially a salesman FOR the company.

You want your new people to talk about the company don't you?

Company Benefits
List all the details about the benefits package here.

In this booklet don't address the 'How To' of accessing the benefits. These should appear in your Operations Handbook - for the simple reason that they will probably change as the company grows.

The Operations Manual is designed to be updated. This booklet is not. Pick what it should include from this list and add anything missing that's appropriate for your company:

- Official working hours
- After hours work policy
- Overtime
- Flexitime
- Public Holidays observed by the company
- Company position on religious holidays
- Vacation arrangements
- Study leave
- Compassionate leave
- Maternity and Paternity leave
- Health Benefits/Dental Plan
- Mortgage relief
- Pay arrangements
- What about pay at Christmas or prior to a plant shut-down period?

- Nursery/crèche arrangements
- Ride share programs
- Work related studies reimbursement
- Professional memberships
- Travel arrangements while on company business
- Visa arrangements for any foreign work
- Arrangements for tax-free status for staff working abroad
- Company Credit Card
- Corporate sponsorship
- Dress code
- Uniforms
- Laundry of corporate uniforms
- Occupational Health and Safety
- Equal Opportunities

Operations Manual

You may think you have no need of an Operations Manual.

Think about how many times people ask how to do something. You and your managers and the rest of your staff can be saved a whole lot of repetitive answering if the key things are written down for everyone to follow.

In our One Day Professional Learning Course 'A Guide to Company Operations' we work with you to draft one that fits your company so you emerge with an outline specific to your own needs. You can do so with your own team.

Standard Operating Procedures will also ensure that when emails and letters go out, all your company documents have the same appearance – a look of efficiency. Many fast growing companies install the standard formats on everyone's computers under speed keys.

Filing - physical and virtual
Virtual

Vital shared folders need to have a home so that in the absence of the author or key user, others can access the information. This SharePoint or equivalent needs to be logically laid out.

Draft the layout on paper first and then create your tree of directories and sub directories and key folders. Decide on access levels and apply them but ensure there is some sort of central online help mechanism for access. If necessary, limit access according to need.

Physical - the filing cabinet

What about the times you have been looking for something filed in someone's filing cabinet when they were absent?

Filing is the most personal of black arts. Who knows how we all create systems that mean something to us?

What if there was an index? What if we could look on the side of the Filing Cabinet and there in a plastic pocket was the current list of files in each drawer?

What if your Virtual Filing Cabinet in the great beyond also had a map so you didn't get lost- and everyone used the same map?

Perhaps you have secure information and don't want these files listed on the side pocket for all to see. You don't want to create what is called by insurance companies 'An Attractive Nuisance' – something that almost invites transgression. In these few cases, still create a list but maintain it in a secure place that is accessible to all who hold the appropriate level of security.

There is a simple system that enables you to log mail. It does presuppose that someone will diligently process all incoming mail and make daily entries into the log. It comprises a simple spreadsheet or table where all incoming mail is listed. The spreadsheet should list

- DATE RCVD
- FROM (Person/Company)
- LETTER DATE
- REGARDING
- ACTION (To whom it was routed)
- FILED (Location - with filing cabinet number of hard copy - or precise digital location). Note that not all documents need filing but be precise about the definition of what must be saved and filed.

Keeping this monthly record can make finding errant documents a lot easier. It also allows someone in the company to check that incoming mail is being handled within the expected period allowed for turnaround of responses. It is also a legally defensible system should you ever get into a testy discussion about what you received, and when.

Tie this to the system of having a master list of how things are filed and you have a ghost's chance in hell of being able to have some consistency in how things are filed company-wide.

Here is an example of how such a list would be numbered:

100	HR general
101	Staff files
101.1	Admin
102	Production
103	Manufacturing

In an exploding growth company there will be times when you need information out of usual business hours.

You need to be able to find what you need, when you need it. Virtual or physical - plan to! One night after a harrowing series of events when you may need to get a document out /do some critical 'before meeting research'/ check your facts before making a critical decision - you will thank your stars that you did.

Standard Operating Procedures

Standard Operating Procedures are there to ensure that the few things that really MUST be done in the same manner every time are done in the same manner every time. This is not every activity in the company! Keep to as few as is possible.

There are numerous reasons why your Operations Manual should let everyone know the way the scaffolding is lashed in your company. These Standard Operating Procedures or SOPs should be reviewed by people in relevant positions at least annually, but whenever an SOP changes. There should be a Change Management SOP that shows how.

The primary reason for this is that if you document it once and set it up on everyone's computer, you can be saved a whole lot of explaining, correcting, and embarrassment.

Here is a list from which you can select content. Add what is missing. *Hopefully select few and delete most.*

- Reception procedures
- Telephone answering
- Long distance calls
- International calls
- Internet access and use
- Booking a teleconference
- Arranging a net meeting
- Mobile phone arrangements
- Standard formats
    - Letters
    - Faxes
    - Order Entry
    - Envelopes
    - Reports
    - Meeting minutes
    - Memos
    - Filing Cabinets
  - Mail handling

- o Mail in
- o Mail Out
- DX or Special delivery
- DHL, UPS, FedEx or other Courier service
  - o Packages
  - o Registered delivery
  - o International Mail
- Fax handling
- Email procedures
- Filing and archiving documents
- Secure storage of sensitive documents
- Corporate confidentiality
- Hiring a car for company business
- Booking accommodation on company business
- Catering arrangements for visitors meetings
- Catering arrangements for internal meetings
- Presentation Kit
- Meeting Kit
- Use of company equipment
- Individual SOPs for specific activities
- Change Management
- Security of access
- Security of company information
- Car parking arrangements
- Corporate sponsorship
- Employee benefits
- Media spokesperson
- Workplace IT SOPs (These are not the technical SOPs that your IT team will operate under, but those meant for office staff: where to store your own data and how so it doesn't get lost in system updates, backup arrangements, storage of large graphic files etc) and media relations

Less is more

Mies van der Rohe[64]

---

[64] Mies van der Rohe, Le Corbusier, Walter Gropius and Frank Lloyd Wright are widely thought to be the founders of modern architecture.

Chapter Fourteen

Good balance:

Safe working inside your bamboo scaffolding

*The trick to forgetting the big picture
is to look at everything close up.*

Chuck Palahniuk[65]

Sustain the people

Now you have the right people in place, the company is growing like an English spring garden on steroids and you want to keep this team intact: it's a good one. Furthermore, you don't have time to keep replacing people.

How do you keep things together?

We suggest you have a goal of doing whatever it is that you have done before that's worked so well. But now you're growing, you need to be aware that changed dynamics mean that everyone is not able to congregate around three desks and have the whole thing evolve. It's going to take some planning. You want your teams to know they are valued. You want them to have fun together, to feel they own the company.

Company meetings? (Groan).It's a universal response. Dry, dusty, self serving and boring would be some of the more generous descriptions. But what if they were not?

What if, every 4 or 6 months you got everyone together - **everyone** – with a replacement reception staff (who have been properly trained by 'The Reflective Receptionist' learning programme) taking the front line for the day and your clients and suppliers advised ahead.

What if, when they came together, they actually had a riotous good time, were shown that they really were valued, and found out from the other divisions what they are up to and how things can marry together better? But how? This was one of my first challenges: brighten up the

---

[65] Chuck Palahniuk is an American novelist, author of Award winning novel 'Fight Club' on which the movie was based.

company meeting. My MD said they were so boring they almost put him to sleep, and it was his company!

I enquired about the budget. What did he have in mind? I was told to keep it reasonable but do something to get everyone interested again. "Hire Concorde and zoom in amongst the buildings," he said. This was a desperate man. Oh and by the way, we had just slightly more than a beer budget for these champagne illusions.

We took all the staff to a country hotel and everyone could either stay over in shared accommodation (i.e. not a room to oneself but shared with a colleague) or take a paid taxi home (within a certain amount of miles). That way no one should drive after drinking.

The first time I decided not to address content, just entertainment. I selected some of the people who were real characters of the company to help design the event to which the staff would emerge at the close of the meeting. They were sworn to secrecy as we concocted a traditional country fair - with a twist. We had:

- A coconut shy (for those who are not English, that is coconuts on precarious holders - you throw a softball at the coconut to knock it off its perch).
- Lucky dips (known as a Grab Bag in the USA) with weird prizes
- Those swivelling clown faces that you try to throw the ping pong ball into their mouths - but they were real people.
- A gypsy fortune teller (who had a beard, so his female disguise was a bit fascinating, but rakish). The fortunes were masterpieces of creativity ,ad-libbed according to the person and accentuated by a pile of props stacked in front of the 'gypsy'.
- A photographer taking sepia-toned photos through an old fashioned camera on a tripod, with costumes for people to dress up in (photos of the design team looking severe and 1800ish, with a caption: "Would you buy a system from these people?" graced their office ever-after)
- A cartoonist (the cartoons were still on the walls when I left the company)

The list was only limited by their inventiveness.

For the next meeting secrecy prevailed despite bribery to wheedle it out of suspected conspirators. This time we also addressed content, and had prizes for the most innovative presentations. These proved strikingly creative and memorable and bore no resemblance to the 'stand-up-and-bore-them' arrangements of the past.

This time the after-meeting-entertainment was a steeplechase with pantomime-horses: two people to a horse costume. We had tyres set out each of the four feet of the horse had to go in a tyre.

There was a water jump made up of several children's inflatable swimming pools, and even a suffragette who threw herself in front of the racing creatures. We had bookies and paper money and lots of silly prizes. A caller introduced the horses and commented on their form as they trotted to the pre-race paddock and then described or 'called' the race.

One of the memorable quotes at the trophy awards was when a junior programmer received his trophy. He thanked everyone, as this was his first ever trophy. He thought it significant that he won it for being the back end of a horse (not quite phrased that way).What I am describing is the building of a corporate character.

This was ours. Yours should reflect the nature of your company but still be creative and sufficiently unconventional that it gets people's attention.

You want people to know what is going out without boring them witless... and by now you know my remedy - get some of your staff together over lunch!

A corporate ethos is a strange thing. It develops out of the stories a company tells about its senior staff and about itself. When it is good, it is treasured.

People aspire to connect with something of character. We live in a grey, faceless corporate world.

Be colour!

Be vibrant, or pastel, but be colourful in whatever measure suits the character of your company.

*Your staff and the market will respond
to a company with personality.*

What about your operations arrangements? Do you have an outline of how things should happen and expect people to be honourable? It's remarkable how often they are, when treated this way.

We had a lot of people from South Africa, New Zealand, and Australia working for us at our London base. I knew that the time zones suggested that the best time for them to call home was when they were at work. As an international company, we had no call-barring on international calls.

When they were hired, all staff were told if they made personal calls long distance they knew roughly how much it would cost. They were told that naturally we could check the bills and have a pretty good idea of who made what call. But we were a small and growing company and didn't expect to pay for their personal long distance calls, so would appreciate them going to the Accounts Department every now and then to pay for their own calls. They did. Unprompted.

Our focus was not on small petty savings, but on things of substance, the pivotal things that make the company go ahead with financial surety or not.

Then, of course are the tragedies.

Who has discretionary power in your company to handle the unexpected? Remember we mentioned the Company Aunt or Uncle?

Contractors are paid on an hourly rate. Don't work: don't get paid. No benefits. That's why they get paid higher hourly rates. We had a contractor working for us who was coming back from an international posting and was to be met at the airport by his family. There was a terrible accident as they travelled to get him. Two of the children were killed, along with his wife. My MD set the precedent for all that we did in the future for employees in distress.

We had no legal obligation to pay this contractor for all the lost time at work he had to spend sorting this out and re-establishing his life. But we had a moral obligation. This is what was honoured. He was on full pay for over a year and came to work when he could.

It goes back to what we said before about rent-on-earth. It's not only the right thing to do, it's good business. If you honour your commitments, you instantly stand out in a world where avoiding responsibility is taken to an art form.

An unexpected result was that word spread: we could take our pick of contractors all across Europe at a time when the skills we sought were hard to come by.

Give someone you trust the authority to make similar right decisions to creatively assist your own people when life rains misfortune on their head. This, too, is part of the ethos. Don't just say you value your people. Show you do.

You do? So what sort of toilet paper is in the 'loo then for your staff? The harsh stuff or the soft stuff? Coffee? Cheap and nasty, or proper coffee with flavour? Free, or are you 'cost saving'? If you are, and it is the accountant who suggested it - get a new accountant who will focus on cost savings that are significant but don't constrain the business or its future. Surprisingly, not providing coffee for employees may do just that because it indicates pettiness, not fiscal responsibility. Birthdays? Any other recognition that is personal?

If your company is German - a word of warning: Don't mess with the car policy unless it's an improvement. Your staff take their cars seriously and a good car policy can make you stand out. Fiddle with it at your own risk. The results are predictable: you'll lose some good people fast.

These are all the messages you are giving to your staff daily; don't underestimate their power.

People talk to me, probably because I talk to them. I'm visibly excited when they tell me of their personal triumphs. I used to take some of these to the MD and let him know about them. He would poke a head through their door and say "I hear that you... Well done!" The effect was like watching light bulbs illuminate by spontaneous energy.

It would be unreasonable to expect him to have the ear of all the employees: that was my job. But his willingness to respond to my carefully chosen list of personal achievements of his staff from their activities outside the office was key in developing our company culture.

Let your staff value you, and chide you in an acceptable fashion. Find ways to diffuse things by making it acceptable for there to be a quiet swipe at the Management Team, or at some practice that the company has unwittingly instituted.

Be yourself. So the way you do things doesn't match anything in a management book -even this one? Does it work?

A former government leader inherited a massive deficit in funds and a subsequent down grading of the credit rating of his government. He had to rebuild fast. All operations review meetings were held standing up.

This included progress reports on new developments that involved nongovernment people. No one was disparaging about it, for they recognised the message. The place was exploding with growth and there's only so much time in a day. This was business and the format of the meeting endorsed the changes from what was perceived formerly to be slow moving, indecisive government. The erosion of business confidence lessened and the economy improved. However, demonstrating something that you also may be susceptible to doing, the new leader later believed his own press about how good he was. He was not re-elected.

Have some fun.

I think that you have that message by now!

But just to reinforce it.

Work out the ways you and the various teams that constitute your company can have fun together while getting the work done. Don't stifle high jinks unless they are of the dangerous variety that has no thought for property, person, or sense of occasion, and please recognise that fun is something spontaneous not something orchestrated.

Humour is a valuable fuse in a fast growing company.

Let's take the saga of the System Development Cat. One day in total frustration, the System Development Manager said she needed a cat to kick. Two days later a hand-sewn black cat appeared on her desk. With relish the cat was kicked. When things went wrong, the cat could be seen from the offices across the court-yard, flying from one boot to the next. One memorable day frustration was unbearable until the cat got kicked and then hung out the window by its tail to torment the cat lovers (who were the source of the frustration) in the overlooking offices.

I was about to leave on a trip overseas and walked into the photocopy room to see a rather embarrassed highly paid contractor huddle over something I was obviously not supposed to see. He confessed and agreed to show me, but only as I was leaving the office for a week or so and therefore couldn't blow his cover. Never mind that I hired and fired!

Carefully cut out letters were being pasted onto a page as a ransom note for the cat. I dreaded to think of the time invested and what that represented for his rate of pay but recognised the frustration behind it and the silliness of the solution. The two teams had been working horrific hours towards a particular goal. There had been a recent glitch causing extensive re-work.

In my absence the cat was duly taken hostage and the note presented in its stead: "If you ever want to see your pussy alive again (with photo of the cat with a water pistol to its head) leave 200 Mars Bars in a grocery bag in Reception by 2pm".

It was the heat of the IRA terrorist attacks in London. The department concerned bravely announced they didn't deal with terrorists. They wouldn't pay.

Photos appeared from all around Europe as the cat travelled with teams to Italy, Germany, France, and even South Africa. Each photo came with a plea for payment and the cat in various threatening situations, often hanging from a tie round its neck in front of a well-known monument.

Christmas arrived. The last present out of Santa's sack was – in the spirit of 'Goodwill Unto Man' – the Development Cat. It was ceremonially kicked by all who stayed up in the bar till in the early hours.

The next week, the leader of the Hostage-Taker group met the MD in the hall. She told him as they passed that she was really distressed at him. He was shocked and enquired why. She responded that she had heard that he had also kicked the cat. "Tell me it's not true!" she said, in mock horror.

He replied instantly "It's not true at all. I did not kick the cat. I dropkicked the cat". The surrounding staff collapsed in fits of laughter.

New Year saw the hostage takers welcome a new arrival: a duplicate cat. It arrived with a full cat-house all nicely quilted and complete with scratching post to take up residence in the window overlooking the offices of the Development Team. This cat was NOT to be kicked. Animal rights signs abounded, facing the sadists across the way.

Predictably, after a rough development run on a new system version, this cat also disappeared. There were dark rumblings, but no one would confess.

A sign went up by the cat house "Ground floor flat with a view to rent". Tins of cat food were stacked beside the sign, tempting tenancy.

One night I was working late and popped into this office to leave something for the manager. The MD, also working late, heard my laughter and asked what was causing it. I brought him to see: On the desk was the missing cat with - a kitten.

The mystery was solved! Yellow Post Its cut in balloon shapes and attached to their mouths carried a tale. The kitten was saying "Mummy, where's Daddy?" and the big cat was responding: "Daddy's done a runner".

At that moment the MD said something that showed that he understood that an exploding growth company needs outlets for its growth frustrations.

"I sure hope someone is keeping a record of this saga. It shows how to let off steam acceptably." After all these years, here it is. Of the many I have seen in my career, I think it one of the best examples of that strange evolution called company ethos where 'work hard' and 'play hard' go together – often as innocently as this.

In whatever form your nonsense arrives – cut it some slack.

It may be the cheapest growth medium
that you will ever be able to employ
for showing where the tensions lie and easing them.

Direct the directors

You got this far with your directors making it up as you went along. Why should you do anything differently?

The answer to that may well be that you need do nothing. Yet. But there will come a time when your team needs a fuse too.

You got this far because you understood the business.
But this is a new business. This business is rocketing off the charts before your eyes. It needs different skills in its direction. It needs you all to act differently than you did before, when it was small and more manageable. Some of the methods of the past may not work for the problems of today.

If you have several offices, you need to get them together and make sure they are all working for the same company. Remember the exercise at the beginning about describing the company?

We are not going to suggest how you do this. Just that you do it. You may get someone outside the company to look at what your growth status is, and make some suggestions.

You may want to just book someone who holds experiential training courses for director level management. Then, have them design a short weekend away programme that addresses your needs. So they can do so, describe where you are and where you are headed. Explain some of the recent potential impediments you see from the top and amongst your directorship team. It may be that you just describe some symptoms without trying to diagnose causes.

Directors generally exhibit no desire to stop and take stock. They're too busy, know what they are doing and don't need any help, thank you very much. Which just shows that someone better make sure you're all looking in the same mirror. A weekend spent learning who you all are as people, and how you think and act is the best investment you'll make.

I'm allergic to hypothetical situations in training. I think they insult what intelligence I have. It's predictable where I am being led so I have a tendency to throw a wobbly in there by doing something unexpected, just to see what will happen. I am not being nasty: just bored. No wonder I had to sit in the front row so often in school.

My dislike of these programs has helped when I have had to design them myself. When I design such a program the elements in common are:

- They're housed in somewhere utterly lovely to be (since the people attending have given up precious family time to be there – usually very grudgingly).
- The activities take place in the outdoors, requiring people to be surrounded by nature.
- They also must encompass some activity that has some meaning. One time it was measuring water levels in various creeks and rivers that the regional water authority wanted but couldn't afford to do. There are lots of examples of such things.
- Their accomplishment requires real-life snap decisions and an element of calculated risk, clear directions from the leader of the exercise, and other actions applicable to work life.

The look on the face of a Director who had been voted team leader for that day when the group arrived to meet their transport after following compass directions across country and found a helicopter and not the expected van was, I am told, worth seeing. The designated leader for that day had just not quite told the entire story to the team. This was his habitual method of maintaining control: he always kept a little bit of crucial information just to himself. As he was airlifted away from the group with the instructions he had elected not to share still in his head and not transferred to the group, he knew he'd left his peers in a real mess.

The team didn't have the necessary information to find their way back across country on foot to where the van awaited. But they regrouped quickly and made an informed guess. They were right, but the point was well made about the difference between real leadership and control.

In such a setting you can make a point very effectively by providing circumstances where individuals can demonstrate to themselves that their usual way of acting may not be suitable. Often such people think themselves warm, empathetic people who are good managers. Once provided with a big mirror such as the helicopter experience, they are suitably horrified by what they have just seen in themselves – and this is reinforced by some not very happy colleagues.

The helicopter scene was set in the anticipation of just this sort of control by withdrawal of relevant information. This behaviour had been stopping the company being able to go ahead smoothly. Directors held key information close rather than being collaborative. We had to find a way for it to be addressed.

You may know when the time comes for such work with your Directors. Maybe you won't. Maybe the other members of your team will. Perhaps you are the one who doesn't divest enough control for them to be able to contribute effectively.

Do you dare to check every six months about how your management team is doing? You should. Your staff will tell you - and they just might say you are the worst offender.

As Isaac Asimov said in 'I, Robot':

It is the obvious that is so difficult to see most of the time.
People say 'It's as plain as the nose on your face.'
But how much of the nose on your face can
you see unless someone holds a mirror up to you?

You need to plan management time-outs at least once a year. This is time to face each other about the frustrations, about the impact from differences of style – about the future and how together you'll face it. This isn't strategy setting, it's people stuff: why you rub me up the wrong way, and how I can find an acceptable way to tell you, and let us together find what we can do about it.

This aspect of your company development is the most sensitive. There is usually someone in the company at a senior level who will tell you what is really happening, and not what you think is happening. Use that person – or a series of such people – as a barometer of your own behaviour and that of your senior team. Use their insight and get your Directors steering together. But beware of false prophets who may have an agenda of their own, or unrealistic expectations, or those who may have a personal reason for scoring points against another.

And get your sticky paws off the oars
when the crew is trying to row!

Plan for when things go wrong

Do you have a plan for when things go wrong? Of course not. You're in the 'Go-Ahead' business, not the 'Hedge-Your-Bets' business. But all business needs to have some room for flexibility.

The best flexibility is that of having staff so attuned to the company, to its ethos, its elemental essence, that when things really go awry, together you can address the situation.
Not all things need the input of all the people, but some do. Radical market shifts are such an example.

You may be amazed at the gold on the work room floor when you need a realistic view of market position and new opportunity.

Awards and Rewards

Unexpected appreciation is always so wonderful.

When someone does something worthy of comment, let them know. Celebrate the good, the silly, the disastrous, and the costly - equally.

Of course any sort of reward system is useless if the people who work in your company have no faith in you, or in the ethics or direction of the company – or if you have demonstrated that you are mouthing the words but they are empty of actions to match.

Let people know that you know the pressures they are under and that you understand that they are making decisions based on the best information to hand at the time.

Remember Rule Number 2?

> ### Rule Number 2:
> It is an unwritten law of ratios that the more things
> a person does, the more mistakes are likely to be
> made by that person, *therefore:*
>
> The person making the most mistakes may not be
> the biggest dolt but instead the high achiever.

Your awards and rewards can be silly and funny, small trophies constructed from telling bits of this and that. The Magnifying Glass with a small disc attached proclaiming a Super Sleuth sat on the desks of many proud winners of our Murder Mystery awards.

The point of these is that they quantify the fact that you recognise the foibles, the faults, the errors, and the achievements that make up the employee as a person – and you see them as a friend would – objectively with all flaws, but still valued. These are the small tributes that mean so much.

Contrary to most management training, complimenting people for their efforts when they are just doing their job as they would normally do produces a counter-intuitive effect. Research[66] shows that praise for good everyday work had a lower effect than statements showing a genuine interest in the person's approach to their work. Comments that do so have much greater impact because they show more than a cursory interest. Research demonstrates that they spur even greater achievement.

Praise used sparingly works best.

There are many ways to show appreciation and the most powerful of all is an interest in your team members as individuals.

In all the time I spent interviewing job candidates throughout my career (and in one two year period we hired 200 – so I interviewed many more than that while still doing my day job) I never met one person who was leaving the current role purely because of the money.

People leave companies because they felt unappreciated.
Find things to celebrate and do so in an even-handed fashion.
Let your own people know they are valued.

---

[66] With thanks to a page from Glasgow University Psychology Dept: Dweck, C. S. (2007).The Perils and Promises of Praise. Educational Leadership, 65(2), 34-39.

Share the wealth.

With growth comes increased wealth. Business needs require that you reinvest it as fast as you make it. But at some point there is a bit left over: quite a bit.

It might be that you don't have a share-ownership plan or a profit-share plan. It might be that you prefer to put aside a percent of the profits (you note I said profits) to take the company and their families somewhere special.

Consider this idea. One Canal Boat Hire company in the early days of the introduction of the Value Added Tax (VAT) in England put the funds due for VAT into a special account. Since they only paid the money out to the government every three months it created a considerable investment fund that would not otherwise have been there. The interest on this over a year paid to take the staff and their partners by coach from the Midlands to 'The London Palladium' (the sort of famous place one aspires to go to) for a grand Christmas celebration: practically cost neutral.

It may be that you reward your sales people with a no ceiling earnings plan balanced by the agreed limits of production capability.

You don't? You don't want them to earn lots? If they earn lots, it comes from having made lots of sales doesn't it?

Allowing for capacity to handle the production of increased orders, more sales equal more money doesn't it? Why are you capping the enthusiasm of your sales team by capping their earnings?

This goes hand in hand with an expectation that you have some method of making sure the sales team sells realistically and not so it stretches the company and its teams to dizzy distraction by promising the unachievable.

And what about the people who constitute the support infrastructure? Should everyone get a percentage share of the gains if they all pull together?

However you do it, share the wealth with the people who helped create it, and – remember triple bottom line?

Share it with your community and the environment as well.

Budgets

Do you have a line item budget? That means that each category of expenditure has its own allotment and you can't move money between them. So if you save on Stationery, you can't use that to top up Travel, and so on.

*If you want to see real excellence in the use of your budget,
eliminate Line Item budgets.*

Let each department have the amount they had before and allow them to spend it as they need to accomplish their goals. Any savings stay in their own department to be deployed on whatever aspect of their business goals they define.

So there we are. We have all the tools to create a company capable of sustaining Shrapnel Free Explosive Growth.

In six weeks time you are going to re-group and revisit the plan you've designed. In the meantime you'll have thought about how all these plans work in real life and maybe modified them in your note books.

As a group you will decide on the final plan and how to get it into place. We trust that so far, this guide has helped you to think through many of the issues important to keeping the shrapnel away from your rocket as you shoot ever upward.

Remember that in the future there'll come a time when you need to make other decisions: whether to become a big corporate or to stay small and divest some of the current functions - or perhaps whether to sell to another company or investor.

Will you help your staff to form companies of their own as suppliers to you? Think about the sort of supplier you prefer to deal with and then ask yourself that question again.

However you structure your company, many of these prompts and stories will cause you to think through some of the issues before they bite you in the ankle.

*Leaders get out in front and stay there
by raising the standards by which they judge themselves –and by which
they are willing to be judged.*

Frederick W. Smith[67], founder of FedEx

---

[67] "Fred" Smith conceived the idea of a centralised clearing house for packages while at University and refined it as a Marine Ground Controller flying thousands of hours with navy pilots in the Vietnam War. He credits the Marine Corp in teaching him how to treat others and how to be a leader.

Chapter Fifteen

Connecting the dots: Just enough design.

*Simplicity is about subtracting the obvious
and adding the meaningful.*

John Maeda[68]

Lashing your bamboo scaffolding

When we began, we reserved a time six weeks ahead to review our early thoughts and jottings. Now is that time.

When your senior team meets, they will bring their exercise books that have recorded answers to the questions we posed at the outset about what the company should look like, operate, and focus upon. The originally blank facing pages should now have lots of scribbles in them. If they don't, they will shortly.

You will have sent out a reminder a month beforehand, but since you all booked this date when you started there are no valid excuses beyond family tragedy, illness, or being physically stranded somewhere by weather or strikes.

Is there anyone who should be there who wasn't there at the outset? If so, get them up to speed by spending some time going through a quick snapshot of progress to date and giving that person their own exercise book and copy of Shrapnel Free so he or she can answer the same questions as the rest of you.

Planning the workshop day

A week before your meeting:

- Confirm arrangements with hotel, for lunch arrangements, with the one-person-contact you have assigned to be the interface between participants and the outside world for that day, and with the facilitator.

---

[68] In 1999 John Maeda was named by Esquire Magazine as one of the 21 most important people in the 21st century. As a Professor at MIT Labs over 12 years he fostered unusually creative technology crossover. The organisations he later led were recognised for their insightful forward thinking. His best-selling book 'Laws of Simplicity' of 2006 is still a key hand book on effective design: for organisational systems, physical things, technology, or life as lived.

- Have someone physically drive to the venue from the office and back by an alternative main route. The reason for this is to check for construction or road works that are impeding traffic flow. I add this step from my own experience of not having done so. Participants arrived late and grumpy, causing reorientation of the schedule and extra time to ungrump them and create a relaxed and happy beginning atmosphere.
- From all of the above make necessary adjustments to the originally agreed text of your Participant Confirmation email (your key interface person no longer available due to illness or family emergency; change of room or parking arrangements at the venue; warnings about route impediments, etc)
- Send redrafted text for approval of the Facilitator: state that it needs 24 hour turnaround.
- Send out the confirmation to participants.
- Do your own preparation by looking back over the work you did together six weeks ago.

On the day:

You are the host. Act like it and make everyone welcome. If this sort of thing makes you nervous, remember that these people have been with you from the start. If you aren't the type of person to make a fuss, they know that.

They respect you for who you are or they'd have already left the fold. That means you can be confident about being yourself – but nevertheless – make everyone feel that you appreciate their effort in coming. It is an effort. Thinking is always an effort.

After breakfast and PROMPTLY at the starting time previously announced, stand at the front of the room to introduce the Facilitator and explain that she or he will guide everyone through three sections of work:

The Big Stuff: Main organisational decisions

The Small Stuff: Details

The Roadmap: How we'll get there.

That's it. Your job is now done until you thank everyone including the Facilitator at the end of the day.

Work sheets for the workshop:
Benchmarks

These are the measures against which our plan for the future must prove itself. If any action we decide upon today doesn't measure up against these, then it needs re-working or removing from our Action List.

Our future company should:

- Retain its unique company ethos.
- Not be over-constrained by rules but instead empower our people to make decisions within understood boundaries.
- Withstand unexpected change.
- Have a management team who readjust as the company changes.
- Be known as a great place to work.
- Be staffed by people who thrive in growth, aren't destroyed by it and who will survive the multi-tasking sometimes needed when growth outstrips resources.
- Be professional always and respect each other and ourselves (in other words, have a sense of occasion).
- Have a lot of fun
- Be respected for its value in providing things that solve problems and for its integrity.
- Create an indomitable market position within the niche of our sector where we operate (that is- focus on core business and not try to be all things to all people).
- Have a supply chain that reflects our values.

The Big Stuff: Main organisational decisions
- What market need do we solve?
- What do we do that is unique?
- What will be the company:
    - Look and feel
    - Style
    - Character
    - Ethos

What we need to accomplish
- In the next 3 months?
- In the next 6 months?

Who do we need
- Right now?
- In 6-12 months?

How will we
- Deal with the unexpected?

- Handle failure?
- Share the wealth?

As a leadership team what do we need to:

- Change?
- Be better at?
- Be consistent about – collectively and as individuals.

The Small Stuff: The details.

We already worked through all the small details or we couldn't have finalised the Big Stuff.

Much of what we need to do on our Action Plan will be done by others.

> *As leaders our job is not to row but to steer.*
> *That means setting out the clear lanes*
> *in which our rowers can row*
> *without bumping into each other*
> *or going over rapids they didn't know were there.*

- As it is our job to steer, how will we impart the Big Stuff to the rest of the team?
- Who outside this team will have responsibility for what, and who on this team will be their touch point?

Before you include the rest of the team there are some steering decisions to be made so everyone is rowing the same course. These are the framing decisions for some of the Small Stuff.

The Precise Stuff: Define.

- The seven things (or fewer) that you do need rules about

A clue here is the way a major airport measures its success. An airport is a city. No one is going to read a rule book for a city. Therefore they trust their staff to act appropriately to ensure an affirmative answer to three measures:

   o Are people safe?
   o Is the place clean and tidy?
   o Are people happy?

Perhaps that is the sort of Operations manual you need. You may need a bit more – knowing the boundaries will mean no one should embarrass your customers, supply chain or collaborative partners, themselves, you, or the brand by extending their discretion beyond the reasonable.

- A process for producing the THIN Operations Manual of things that must be done in a certain way and the boundaries of those

where there is considerable discretion: budgetary limits may be one such measure.
- A rewarding career path for technical people apart from management.
- The peak periods in a year when any sort of structural remodelling should not take place, if at all possible.
- Contractor hiring policy.
- Supply chain selection and management.
- If, and if so how, other companies can collaborate in bundling your products and/or services with theirs.
- How innovation is actively encouraged, how it is recognised and acted upon when developed 'on the shop floor', and what the rewards are for your team in doing so.
- Any particular aspect of your operations that is 'mission critical'. Then add it to your benchmarks under a heading *'Mess with this at our peril'*.

The Roadmap: How we'll get there.

Given all the answers you have worked to agree upon – decide what is:
- The 30/60/90 day action plan
- The budget, if required
- The person responsible for seeing that each action is done within time and budget
- How you will measure success of each action: this is not to measure activity but result!
- The communication plan so others participate in developing your bamboo scaffolding so they recognise it for what it is.

They can then tell you the points where you need to lash the structure more tightly or loosely; alert you to unidentified hazards and can tell others outside the company the message you want to be told, not the one they make up because from where they sit it seems plausible.

Now you and your team can get busy steering and stop trying to row: grabbing the oars from those who were doing well at it before being interrupted.

Change is often necessary but never easy and too often misinterpreted. Keep a light hand on the sails. You can't do anything about the winds of change but you can adjust your sails. The work you have done together should leave you able to stop worrying about steering the fast-moving super yacht your company has evolved into, and let all of you feel more comfortable about facing a future defined by growth and all its challenges.

You will have to revisit this process in a year or so, but by now it should be second nature and much faster. You are so much better prepared and are now set to a future of your own design, not to reacting to that of others. After considering your answers to some of these questions, you'll have created a firmly lashed, flexible structure – scaffolding on which you can safely scramble around in any weather and feel shrapnel free. Inside it, the company will be evolving and taking on its individual characteristics. In doing so, it will create a unique ethos that will be treasured forever after by all those who are part of the exciting, maddeningly frustrating, exhilarating ride to the top.

Good luck and may you be able to sigh in relief with sound bamboo scaffolding within which to grow.

Shrapnel Free Explosive Growth can be managed but it needs you to guide it.

I end with this advice from American President Calvin Coolidge:

Nothing in the world can take the place of Persistence.

Talent will not;
nothing is more common than unsuccessful men with talent.

Genius will not;
unrewarded genius is almost a proverb.

Education will not;
the world is full of educated derelicts.

Persistence and Determination alone are omnipotent.

The slogan "Press On"
has solved and will always solve the problems of the human race.

Index

Lightning Source UK Ltd.
Milton Keynes UK
UKHW01f0626090818
326985UK00002B/55/P